"This book is an antidote to both the cynicism that has poisoned politics for so many Americans and the skepticism that too many feel about religious communal life in our society. Theirs is a refreshing story of political idealism, relevant spirituality, and sacred service. Of course, at the end of the day it is a love-story. Joyce and Steve's story is a call to all of us (Jewish or not) to be our best selves."

Rabbi Jonah Dov Pesner, Director Religious Action Center of Reform Judaism and Senior Vice President Union for Reform Judaism

"If you want to learn how a remarkable couple can engage deeply in their community, and thrive, we should read *The Rabbi and Senator Sleep Together*. I have known and worked with Steve and Joyce Foster for decades and their lives have been 'profiles in courage'. As a former Mayor of Denver, I could always count on the Fosters standing up against prejudice, tackling difficult challenges, and fashioning constructive solutions to divisive issues. They have never hesitated or wavered in the face of controversy or criticism. We can all learn from their lives and experiences and our community is truly better because of their enormous contributions."

Federico Pena, former Denver Mayor and U.S. Secretary of Transportation

"For those who have a passion for serving others *The Rabbi and Senator Sleep Together* is a must read. Strong advocacy along with a genuine respect for those who may disagree has guided the path of Rabbi Steven and Senator Joyce Foster. In the process, they have aided all of us in learning how to make a difference in our own lives."

Hank Brown, former: U.S. Senator (R-Colo.) and president of the University of Colorado and University of Northern Colorado

"We shared the same interest; we fought for the same principles."

Wellington Webb, former Denver Mayor

"Rabbi Steven Foster and Senator Joyce Foster, dear friends and colleagues, have written a wonderful account of their lively relationship beginning with their 'love at first sight' and continuing through their retirement memories. Their leadership, humor, love of family and friends, and, above all, their dedication to the synagogue and to the quality of life in the city of Denver and the state of Colorado are richly chronicled and engagingly recounted. They deserve unending gratitude for their contributions to making the world a better place for us all, and for adding this memoir as a reminder of how marital and familial love can be a foundation for wise leadership and enduring contributions."

Larry Kent Graham, Emeritus Professor of Pastoral Theology and Care at the Iliff School of Theology

"Rabbi Steve Foster and Senator Joyce Foster have been wonderful friends to me for many years. Their passion for their community, public service, and social justice issues is unsurpassed. Throughout their over 50 years of marriage, they have taught their children, grandchildren and those of us who are lucky to have them as friends the meaning of love, friendship and giving back to their community and the country. In my own journey of public service as Colorado Attorney General, United States Senator, and Secretary of Interior, Steve and Joyce have inspired and guided me with their wisdom and example. I wholeheartedly endorse their wonderful biographical work and hope that others will learn of their rich history and giving spirit."

Ken Salazar, former: U.S. Secretary of the Interior,
U.S. Senator (D-Colo.) and Colorado Attorney General

"For as long as I can remember Steven and Joyce Foster have been quiet – and sometimes not so quiet – advocates for justice and fairness. They were there when I had my philanthropic 'coming out' two decades ago and they are there today always pushing for people to do the right thing. The world is a better place because of their efforts. They are a reminder to us all that you must think smarter, think bigger and never stop in pursuit of your goals."

Tim Gill, LGBT rights activist (lesbian, gay, bisexual and transgender),
philanthropist and computer software entrepreneur

"For five decades, Rabbi Steven and Senator Joyce Foster have spent their lives giving back to their community and family. They both have taken leadership roles fighting for social justice issues and bringing different segments of the community together for real change. Their book chronicles these achievements and also offers helpful advice for politicians and clergy. They stand as fine examples of what politicians and clergy should strive to achieve."

U.S. Senator Michael Bennet (D-Colo.)
and former superintendent of Denver Public Schools

"I learned a lot from Steve over the years about Israel and contemporary Jewish life. We could disagree but it was important to have the conversation with Steve and learn from him. He is a leading light in Jewish education in America and an important voice."

The Very Rev. Peter Eaton, former Dean of Saint John's Cathedral in Denver,
current Bishop Coadjutor of the Episcopal Diocese of Southeast Florida

The Rabbi and Senator Sleep Together

Marrying Religion and Politics

by *Rabbi Steven and Senator Joyce Foster*

with Cindy Brovsky

TRIPLE D PRESS

DENVER

For information or to order additional copies, contact
Triple D Press
8239 E. 5th Ave.
Denver, CO 80230
tripledpress@gmail.com
therabbiandsenatorsleeptogether.com

LCCN 2015913286
ISBN 978-0-69251053-7 – Paperback
ISBN 978-0-692-53619-3 – EPUB
ISBN 978-0-692-53620-9 – MOBI

Production Management by
Paros Press LLC
P.O. Box 22255   Denver, CO 80222
303-472-0099   www.parospress.com

Book Design by
Scott Johnson

Printed in the United States of America
First Printing

We dedicate this book

to our families – past and present –

whose love and support make us

the people we are today.

We carry you in our hearts

every day.

Introduction

An old saying admonishes us to never discuss religion and politics in mixed company. Well, for us, religion and politics have been front and center in our marriage and throughout most of our adult lives. And that is not a bad thing. In fact, as a couple we believe that religion and politics must intersect where the common good is at stake.

That is not to say we don't strongly believe in the separation of church and state. As Jews, we know that historically, if any country adopts one religion as the state's religion, the Jews are likely to be displaced. We have only to look to our own family histories where our grandparents faced strong discrimination in Eastern Europe and came to the United States to escape anti-Semitism.

We also know firsthand that clergy and politicians are held to a higher standard – rightly so – but that means our lives under the microscope are not always easy.

With Steve's 11 years as the assistant rabbi and 29 years as the senior rabbi of Temple Emanuel in Denver, Colorado and Joyce's 10 years as the first female Jewish Denver City council-woman and four years as a state senator, we are considered a high-profile couple with widespread name recognition. But because of our careers we have only a handful of people we consider our true friends, and we know other clergy and politicians feel the same way about their circle of friends.

We were at every bar and bat mitzvah at the temple, but often our two sons and daughter wouldn't be invited – which bothered Joyce.

> Joyce: "They saw us as the clergy, not as a family, and that was a tough, tough issue. I am sure that's true whether you are a rabbi or minister. My heart would just break when I saw everyone's kids, and our children were not invited – especially when they introduced us as their 'dearest friends' to their guests."

But our children never felt slighted.

"You know that's why our parents were always each other's best friend," said our oldest son, David. "Not going to another bar or bat mitzvah was always fine with us. I imagine that's what my mom was most disappointed in: the constant reinforcement of the fact that people weren't as close as my parents thought they had been."

We have faced the challenges of growing our congregation and garnering votes and the often difficult and sometimes humiliating task of raising money for political campaigns and the synagogue.

We have sometimes alienated our congregation or constituents when they disagreed with us, but we stood up for what we believed and we never backed down. We've lived by the code: "Principle before politics."

> Steve: "This is something we have in common as a rabbi and a politician. We never pander to anybody. We stand up for what we believe in."

We know when to do the right thing, whether ministering to the mother of one of the Columbine High School shooting suspects shortly after the tragedy or as Denver City Council president sending Denver police first to the Muslim mosque the morning of 9/11 because we needed to make sure their community was safe from possible retribution.

We wanted to write this book because we have taken this unique journey together not only as a husband and wife but as a rabbi and rebbetzin, father and mother, rabbi and city councilwoman, and retired rabbi and retired state senator.

"Growing up in a house where two parents really did live social justice and standing up for others, I always stood up for the kids who got beat up or bullied," said our daughter, Debbie.

We call it "walking the walk" and standing by our convictions. We strongly support civil and gay rights and interfaith dialogue, including leading mixed religious group trips to Israel and reaching out to the Denver Muslim community.

"Steve and I would have lots of conversations about Israel and Palestine and that's how our two journeys began to Israel in 2006 and 2007," said Bill Calhoun, the former pastor of Montview Boulevard Presbyterian in Denver. "I saw Jews and Presbyterians learning a little more about the history and situation and that gave me great joy. Steve also made an effort with the Muslim community. He initiated it as a leader."

Joyce also didn't shy away from difficult issues. One example was when she went to the mat against other elected officials to make sure Denver built a skateboard park for youth and adults after the city made it illegal to skateboard downtown on the 16th Street Mall and other public places.

Rabbi Steven Foster served the Temple Emanuel congregation in Denver for 40 years. Congregate Ron Simon regularly blows the shofar, a horn traditionally made from a ram, during Rosh Hashanah and Yom Kippur. However, Steve took over the honor during one service in the 1980s. (courtesy Temple Emanuel)

"Without Joyce's consistent leadership and consistently resisting the 'Not in My Backyard' pressure, the skateboard park never would have gotten built," said former NFL player Dave Stalls, who ran a center for at-risk youth and young adults. "No question it should be named after her."

Even if people didn't agree with our convictions, they often overlooked what they considered our trespasses because they knew that when they really needed us – whether at a bar mitzvah or funeral or neighborhood planning issue or controversial vote – we were always there ready to serve.

"Rabbi Foster can be polarizing with his thoughts and

Joyce Foster was the first Jewish woman elected to the Denver City Council. She served from 1993-2003 and was elected by her peers as council president from 2001-2002. (photo: Michael Stillman)

opinions but no matter how offended or upset you may be, you always know he is going to give a great funeral," said Jim Cohen, former board president for Temple Emanuel and owner of Feldman Mortuary, Denver's Jewish funeral home. "He doesn't have a stock story. He really knows the person and if he doesn't he spends enough time with the family to deliver the perfect eulogy."

Like a surgeon, police officer, or firefighter, we were on our jobs 24/7 and often picked up a phone call at home late at night or early in the morning. Obviously, not every clergy or public official will be that available and responsive, and many set boundaries. But we didn't.

There were many times Steve was awakened by calls that a member of his congregation was in the hospital, and half-asleep he got up, dressed, and went to the hospital.

> Steve: "And when there were times when I really didn't want to get up in the middle of the night, Joyce would remind me I should get up."

There also were numerous times constituents would call Joyce late in the evening to complain about a pothole or the neighbor's overgrown weeds.

> Joyce: "Sometimes I would be on the phone for a few minutes and sometimes more than an hour. I took the calls."

The typical rules of not bothering someone afterhours often do not apply to clergy or politicians. We felt that was just part of our jobs and met those calls with availability and responsiveness.

But that kind of availability can negatively impact clergy and political families. Popular reality television shows, such as "Preacher's Daughters," paint a gloomy picture of clergy children who rebel with sex, drugs, and leaving their childhood faiths. We know that's a good storyline for TV but also, unfortunately, it's what some clergy families face.

We raised three children in the fishbowl and never had a conventional weekend with the kids. Yet, thankfully, our sons, David and Danny – established attorneys and partners in their own Denver firm, Foster Graham Milstein & Calisher, which employs 30 attorneys – and our daughter, Debbie, a beloved Temple Emanuel preschool teacher and tutor for bat/bar mitzvah, did not rebel against our lifestyles but embraced our legacies.

We're not painting them perfect but we do feel proud all three are kind people with good hearts, good intentions, and commitments to many of the same issues we support.

"If not for my name and the connections I have in this community I wouldn't be where I am today, there's no doubt about that," Danny said. "People know my family's name and for that I was very fortunate."

How lucky are we that David and Ali's three children – Abby, Aiden, and Aaron (Bo) – are growing up within a block of their cousins, Danny and Becky's three children – Rex, Lucy, and Ozzie. Our home and Debbie's condominium are just a few blocks from them.

"I never grew up with first cousins who lived down the street from us," Ali said. "It is pretty incredible in this day and age for all of us to live in the same city and in the same neighborhood."

We feel proud about our accomplishments and appreciate the numerous awards and recognitions over the years. We went from a young clergy couple traveling to conventions to learn more from our elders to setting the national agenda – including how to address interfaith marriages.

Steve served as president of the Denver Rabbinical Council and president of the Midwest Association of Reform Rabbis. He also was co-chair of the national Commission on Outreach for the Reform Movement (a joint effort of the Union of American Hebrew Congregations and the Central Conference of American Rabbis) for 12 years.

He also served on the board of the Rabbinic Cabinet of the Jewish Federations of North America and as chair from 2009-2011.

Steve's work on boards included the National Council of Justice and Peace (formerly the National Conference of Christians and Jews), United Way, and the Allied Jewish Federation, to name a few.

Prior to her election on the Denver City Council, Joyce worked 16 years for Jewish Family Service as director of employment services and assisted Jewish refugees from the former Soviet Union and Pacific Rim countries. She served as president of the city council and pushed for light rail expansion in Denver and addressed long-time needs in her district, including park and shopping center renovations.

We have experience and some wisdom that we hope people who serve the public can relate to and perhaps learn from.

We also feel strongly that if we tell our story it has to be the whole picture. It means lifting the veil that clergy and politicians sometimes wear implying our lives are perfect.

While we "fell in love at first sight" our marriage nearly did not happen. We broke up but were subsequently reunited less than 24 hours later when Joyce received the devastating news that her father committed suicide. Her mother was a widow at 53.

Joyce has spoken candidly about her father's struggle with mental illness, and our daughter, Debbie, is bravely talking about her journey, as well. Any family who has faced mental health issues knows the misconceptions and ignorance that continue to surround the numerous challenges of the disease. Many bright, creative people fear sharing they are bipolar or battling depression for fear of being labeled unstable. Friends and employers often lose patience with the symptoms of the disease – including being late for work, canceling plans, and isolating.

We know individuals and families go through what seems like an endless cycle of looking for the right combination of medications and counseling. And often they are on this roller-coaster alone for fear of judgment.

On the flip side, we know there are many caring people who do not judge or label. But until there is more discussion and understanding of mental illness, the stigma remains.

The tragic suicide of beloved comedian and actor Robin Williams may have helped more people understand that depression can hit anyone – even someone who made us laugh for years. We agree clergy and politicians can help educate about mental health by being compassionate and aware that this is a serious issue for society.

We share the same opinions on most big issues. But like any couple we disagree on different topics and sometimes our passionate conversations raise a few eyebrows. We want to be clear that we know when to stop; words are powerful and can be hurtful.

Being married for 50 years, we obviously agree more than we disagree. What has worked for us is to address something in the moment, and sometimes that adds a little drama to our banter. Joyce says some people refer to us as the "Bickersons," like the couple on the old radio show, when they see us squabble.

To ignore this aspect of our marriage would be dishonest and as we chronicled our memories for this book those exchanges surfaced and will be included throughout these pages.

Readers will also notice that after we bicker we often end the fight with humor – a Foster trait that our children inherited.

We want to show readers that clergy and politicians have real problems and issues just like everyone else. Our daughter-in-law

Becky noted that communication – even if it is arguing – can help a marriage. Otherwise, resentments can build up and ruin a relationship.

"They fight and they argue and they get it out in the open and it's over and done with," Becky said. "It's the rest of us who are uncomfortable sitting around and listening to it but really, it doesn't faze me."

Our good friends, Natalie and Steve Goldman, have witnessed some of our squabbles.

"Steve told me the most important three words in a marriage are: 'Yes, my darling,'" Steve Goldman joked.

Natalie has a different view: "You look at couples who never disagree or bicker and look like a perfect family, and that often ends up in divorce."

Even though at times the public expects clergy and politicians to be super humans, we are not. Sometimes those unrealistic standards crush the very people who should continue to serve.

We hope by sharing our story we help others who have chosen this same path, because the rabbi and senator who sleep together understand the challenges clergy and politicians face.

1

Family Roots

*Grandparents' courage,
love at first sight and tragedy*

To understand someone you have to start at the beginning. Our beginning as a couple was truly love at first sight and the way Steve tells the story reads like a Hollywood script.

Our first conversations were over the phone when Steve was a student at the University of Wisconsin in Madison, already active in the civil rights movement and working at a Jewish summer camp sponsored by the Union of American Hebrew Congregation. It was 1964.

The camp, located in the picturesque community of Oconomowoc between Madison and Milwaukee, attracted many people from Chicago, where Joyce lived. Steve needed the job to help pay his college tuition and raise money to attend the

Hebrew Union College - Jewish Institute of Religion graduate school to become a rabbi.

Steve was born and raised in Milwaukee. A rabbi from his childhood there was inspirational.

Rabbi Herbert Friedman came to Milwaukee's Temple Emanuel from Denver's Temple Emanuel when Steve was about 10. Even though he was just a child, Steve remembers his parents soaking up every sermon from Rabbi Friedman. Many touched on social justice issues. Rabbi Friedman was one of the first religious leaders to criticize Senator Joseph McCarthy's crusade against so-called un-Americans, which unfairly destroyed many people's careers and lives.

Rabbi Dudley Weinberg succeeded Rabbi Friedman after he went on to become CEO of the United Jewish Appeal. Rabbi Weinberg performed Steve's bar mitzvah and was the father of Steve's good friend, Avram.

Seeing such strong Reform rabbis garner the respect of his parents and community influenced Steve's decision to become a rabbi.

> Steve: "Rabbi Friedman took the city by storm and it was a huge deal. He wasn't afraid of anyone. When he left, Rabbi Weinberg came and he wasn't afraid of anyone, either. They had status and influence and they could talk about anything they wanted as long as they couched it in the right way."

Steve's older sister, Syril Newman, remembers that Steve knew he wanted to be a rabbi at a young age. She said even as a baby and young child he emitted charisma, although his personality wasn't always embraced. His third-grade teacher wrote his parents a note that basically said one day someone would put Steve Foster in his place.

By the eighth grade, Steve wrote in a yearbook that his goal was to become the senior rabbi for the Congregation Emanu-El B'ne Jeshurun in Milwaukee. That dream would come true at another Temple Emanuel in Denver.

"He had a beautiful boy soprano voice and on one occasion he was invited to the synagogue in Kenosha [Wisconsin, where his mother's relatives lived] to sing," Syril recalled.

One drawback to singing well surfaced when a teacher at his public school tapped Steve one Christmas to sing "Ave Maria" in a Christmas program. Steve's grandfather, an oppressed Jew who emigrated from Eastern Europe, was appalled. What seemed like a simple thing, for a teacher to pick out the best singer for the performance, felt like a slap in the face for a man who endured discrimination because of his religious beliefs. Here his grandson was, singing a deeply religious Christian song.

Steve sang the song to the shock of his family in the audience. He has little memory of the event other than the story often retold by his family.

> Steve: "I was 7 or 8 years old, just a little kid. I don't remember singing but it was something I was reminded of constantly by my grandfather and my parents. I was a boy soprano, so the teacher thought it was an honor. I think my sister and I were the only two Jewish kids in the school."

Both sets of our grandparents spoke little about their lives before they immigrated to the United States in the early 1900s.

With th
HARVESTER B
SE

What we have been able to cobble together is that the majority of them hailed from an area of Eastern Europe known as the "Pale of Settlement." This basically was a region the Russian Empire had banished Jews to, from 1791 until the fall of the empire to Communism in 1917. It included much of present-day Lithuania, Belarus, Poland, Moldova, Ukraine, and parts of western Russia. Prior to borders and country names being changed, it included the Kingdom of Prussia, later the German Empire, and Austria-Hungary.

of the

MILWAUKEE

2

Steve's grandfather Aaron Zutowsky (second on the right, front row) played the clarinet in Milwaukee after emigrating from Eastern Europe to the U.S. in 1907. Steve has two of his grandfather's clarinets encased and displayed in our home, which will go to our grandson, Aaron "Bo" Foster.

At its height, more than five million Jews lived in the area and their lives were filled with hardships and poverty because of laws prohibiting them from education and commerce. Anti-Jewish riots plagued the communities; many people were killed and much property was destroyed. Between 1881 and 1914, an estimated two million Jews emigrated from the Pale, with the majority coming to the United States.

Of course, our grandparents believed America's streets were paved with gold because that is what they were told before they arrived and found otherwise. But the main reason they came to the U.S. was to escape anti-Semitism in Eastern Europe. They saw the U.S. as a place where Jews could openly practice their religion and for the most part be allowed to pursue an education and financial success.

Steve's paternal grandparents, Aaron and Sarah Zutowsky, first came to Boston and then settled in Milwaukee. The 1920 census lists both of their birthplaces as Russia and that they emigrated in 1907.

The story Steve heard is that before his grandfather arrived in Boston, his name was misspelled on travel documents and the "F" became a "Z" and therefore was listed on documents as Zutowsky. As with many immigrants he never bothered to correct it. However, when Steve's father and uncle were born, Aaron wanted his sons to have the original spelling and changed their last name to Futowsky, even though he and his wife maintained Zutowsky.

When Steve's parents married, his mother took the Futowsky name but she lobbied for a change.

> Steve: "She wasn't thrilled to be going from her maiden name of Buchbinder to Futowsky."

Steve's older sister was born with the Futowsky name. But before Steve came along in 1943, his parents, Milton and Miriam, changed their last name to Foster and that became Steve's last name, as well. The couple already had things

Steve Foster at age 3 holding a pipe and 25 years later smoking one in the 1970s.

engraved with the letter "F." When they were choosing their new name they opened a phone book under the "F" section and landed on Foster. Hence the new family name.

As business owners, they also probably liked Foster because it was less-Jewish than Futowsky. This wasn't an uncommon practice as other Jews and immigrants changed their last names as well because of discrimination.

Steve's family lived in a suburb of Milwaukee known as Fox Point. Their home was modest and the neighborhood was working middle class. But because many other nearby homes were much larger and owned by wealthier families, Steve and his immediate neighbors were viewed as living "on the wrong side of the tracks."

Still, it was an accomplishment that they owned their home considering Steve's father survived a bad business partner and bankruptcy. They had an office supply business and his partner embezzled funds, which led to the bankruptcy. But instead of letting the courts excuse some of the debt, Steve's father spent years paying what was owed. Hence, the family lived in a small home without a garage while Steve's best friend, Mark Stein, whose family lived on the other side of the tracks, had a membership to the country club.

Steve's parents began a printing business that they operated as a couple. Years later Syril, a young mother, and her husband joined the business and they all worked together even when Syril and her husband divorced.

There was no question Steve would attend college and he first went to the University of Wisconsin in Milwaukee and then transferred to Madison. His parents helped with the costs and Steve, a member of a fraternity, washed pots and pans at a woman's dormitory for his meals.

In high school, he worked part-time at a pharmacy as a stock boy and cashier and took other odd jobs to save money for his education. Both of us learned our work ethic at an early age and were expected to be at work on time and without complaining.

In college, Steve began his involvement with the civil rights movement and traveled with fellow students in 1965 to the Selma-to-Montgomery March led by Martin Luther King, Jr. Steve was 22 years old.

Later, as a young assistant rabbi in Denver, he expanded his commitment to civil rights to include the gay and lesbian community.

As a rabbinic student after graduating from Wisconsin, Steve had a part-time position in Union City, Tennessee in

Obion County, which voted overwhelmingly for Alabama Governor George Wallace, a promoter of racial segregation, for President in 1968. Before a Passover Seder in Union City that year after the assassination of Dr. King, Steve asked the congregation to stand and honor King's memory.

Steve: "Right before the Seder began, I asked everyone to stand. They didn't know what they were standing for until I asked for a moment of silence in memory of Dr. King. Well, some of the people who were standing wanted to tar and feather me because some of them were racists. But I didn't hesitate because Dr. King was assassinated just two weeks before and I thought the moment of silence was appropriate."

Joyce: "I think that was really the start of Steve jumping into social justice issues as an individual and student rabbi. He marched in Selma with others, but here he was alone asking others to stand for a moment of silence. And he knew there would be people there who did not agree with him."

Steve: "For me, it was never a tough issue to make the connection between Biblical truth and modern issues. That is who I have been my whole rabbinic career. It was not just politics but was to make the connection between religious truths and what was going on in the world. And yes, when I was a student rabbi – and I was there every other week – it was a testing for me. I never hesitated if there was a social justice issue on my mind. I would raise it on the weekends I was there."

Joyce: "It was miraculous they didn't fire Steve on the spot. But people began listening to him and valued his insights and his courageous convictions."

While Steve's paternal grandparents were dirt poor and came from Eastern Europe, his maternal grandparents, Sigmund and Bessie Buchbinder, were earlier immigrants who had established themselves in Milwaukee. In time, they became wealthy. Census information lists Sigmund's birthplace as Czechoslovakia and Bessie's as Poland. They immigrated to the U.S. in 1885.

Sigmund began his career as a fine woman's tailor and later invested in real estate. Over the years, he owned much of downtown Milwaukee.

The couple had eight children; Steve's mother was the youngest. They grew up in a large home on the east side of Milwaukee before the stock market crash of 1929 eventually caused the family to lose everything except their home and one additional piece of property. In 1930, Steve's grandparents reported to the census that their granddaughter and grandson were living with them along with two female "servants" in their late 20s.

But Miriam Foster's parents had enough money to later try to stop her marriage to Milton. Bessie Buchbinder was so appalled that her daughter was considering marrying a man who grew up in a Jewish ghetto in Milwaukee (just a block from the future president of Israel, Golda Meir) that she whisked Miriam off to Bermuda for six months in the hopes of breaking up the couple. The ploy didn't work and they married when she returned.

Joyce's grandparents settled in Indiana and Michigan. Like Steve, one side of her family was dirt poor (her mother) and another side wealthy before the stock market crash (her father).

Joyce's maternal grandparents, Hyman and Gittel Sclamberg, came from Latvia and Lithuania in the early 1900s.

Hyman lists his birth date as December 5, 1882 on his World War I and World War II draft cards and his birthplace as Russia. He became a naturalized U.S. citizen on May 4, 1909.

Joyce's mother, Beverly, was one of five children and was born in 1911 in South Bend, Indiana. Her grandfather was in the junk business; he had a small truck to pick up scrap metal that he sold.

In contrast, her father's parents, Sam and Sarah Cohn, had a very successful business in Benton Harbor, Michigan, called The Dutch Dry Cleaners. The 1930 census lists both of their birthplaces as Poland and they immigrated to the U.S. in 1899.

Joyce's father, Bill, was one of three sons. As a young adult he was accepted to the prestigious Medill School of Journalism at Northwestern University in Evanston, Illinois but by then money problems plagued the family and his dreams of being a writer were dashed.

Instead, he ended up working odd jobs and driving 38 miles on the weekends from Benton Harbor to South Bend to see his girlfriend, Beverly Sclamberg. Joyce's parents met in 1930, dated and broke up and they didn't reunite and marry until March 25, 1939.

Joyce has a stack of 56 love letters from her father to her mother from October 1930 until July 1931 when they broke up. Bill professes his love for Beverly, who he calls "sweetheart and honey" in the letters. At times he mailed two a day to her. Throughout the correspondence, he says she is his one and only love and asks her to be patient until 1933, at which time he hints they can marry.

"I'm sorry you got hell for coming in so late and I blame myself all day long – but we won't let it happen again (If we can help it.)," he wrote in a December 16, 1930 note.

However, the letters also show a rift with his family's business and at one point he didn't have a job because he "socked" his cousin in the nose. When his father later rehired him, his car was broken down for months and he had to beg friends for rides to see Beverly. One weekend he hitchhiked and another time his friend's car ran out of gas and they pushed the vehicle four miles to get home.

It's clear in the letters that Beverly became upset on the weekends when he didn't show up. On March 31, 1931, Bill wrote that he tore up her letter when she questioned whether he couldn't visit because of a business trip with his father. In his last letter to her, dated July 27, 1931, he broke up with her because he felt she no longer had faith in him.

A few years later, Joyce's Grandfather Sam Cohn, who struggled with mental illness, lost all of the family money and committed suicide. It's unclear if this had any impact on her parents reuniting but they did so, got married and lived in Benton Harbor, where Joyce's sister, Sharon, was born. They later moved to South Bend, where Joyce was born in 1944 and her brother Jack 18 months later.

When Joyce was about 5 years old the family ended up moving to Benton Harbor to be near her father's family. Joyce's grandmother, Sarah Cohn, and uncle, Peter Cohn, both suffered from mental illness and had to be institutionalized. It's a painful memory for Joyce but in those recollections she'll often soften the sadness with a joke.

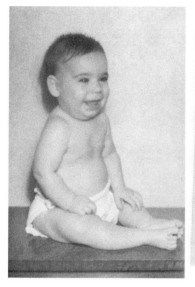

Joyce Foster at age 1. Growing up in Benton Harbor, Michigan. Joyce (far right) with her older sister, Sharon, and younger brother, Jack.

> Joyce: "I mean it was the warehousing of the mentally ill behind lock and key. My grandmother was in the women's side and my uncle was in the men's side. My dad was responsible for my grandmother and uncle and we would visit on Sundays. I mean, didn't everyone go visit their grandma and uncle at a mental institution?"

The things Joyce remembers about those trips to the mental institution in Kalamazoo were the locks on the doors and visiting at picnic tables first with her grandmother at the women's ward and then moving to the men's ward where they saw their uncle Peter. Only one person in Joyce's father's immediate family – his brother, Herman Cohn – did not have mental illness.

"It was a family issue; because the Jewish community all knew each other they knew about it," recalled Joyce's sister,

Joyce's family lived in her father's family home in Benton Harbor, Michigan which was located on Main Street. Her mother, Beverly, turned the garage (far right) into a clothing store.

Sharon Cohn Rubinstein. "My husband called Benton Harbor a Peyton Place because there were no secrets there."

Joyce's parents moved into the family home on Main Street. Once a wealthy neighborhood, the area now was primarily working class and African-American. Her mother came up with the idea to convert their garage into a dress shop that basically was one of the first outlet stores, a precursor to Loehmann's.

> Steve: "During the race riots of 1968 after Martin Luther King was assassinated Benton Harbor was on the national news because of the riots. And they were filming what was going on from my mother-in-law's front porch. It wasn't

a ghetto when Joyce was young but it became a ghetto by the early 1960s."

Joyce's parents bought overstock clothes and accessories that they sold at the store. Their mother already knew the clothing business because she worked at a prestigious department store in South Bend when she was younger and was an accomplished seamstress.

"Our mother came up with the idea of silk-screen T-shirts long before they became popular," Sharon said.

Their parents catered to their African-American customers by learning their common fashion phrases: "ear bobs" were earrings and "a dress with a tail" was a full skirt. They also provided layaway, free alterations and would open the shop if a customer needed something after hours.

The children grew up working in the store and recall many family dinners interrupted because the customers came first.

"I did it reluctantly," Sharon said. "When the bell rang one of us ran into the store."

They never got paid but the girls could choose clothes from the store and on Sundays their father gave them each a dollar to go bowling or for other activities. Jack also remembers them watching "American Bandstand" on TV and Joyce teaching him to jitterbug.

While Joyce's parents worked hard at the store, they struggled to pay the bills and often had creditors after them. Bill Cohn tried several ventures that failed, then went into the fireworks business with another family member.

"We put a fireworks stand in front of our house on Main Street and even though we were a little town we got traffic,"

You can see by our confirmation photographs that Steve grew up in a much larger synagogue in Milwaukee (third from the left, third row) than Joyce (second from the left) in Benton Harbor.

Joyce's brother, Jack Cohn, recalled. "Joyce was probably 9 and I was 7 and we sold sparklers and snakes and other fireworks. Trucks would stop. By the time I was in high school, I was helping our dad with six stands."

The extra money helped pay for family summer trips, Jack said, and eventually financed his college tuition at the University of Michigan, where he earned a teaching degree. After he taught for several years, his family's entrepreneurial spirit kicked in and Jack founded a successful greeting card business that sold to Walmart, Walgreens, and a national craft store.

"We never knew how poor we were," Jack recalled.

But even as a young child, Jack knew his family would find a way to pay for him to go to college.

"Joyce and Sharon were always social and everyone liked them," he said. "I was the serious dude of the three of us. When Sharon went to college my parents had to borrow money from a friend so I knew that was a big deal. When Joyce was ready to go, there was no one to ask to borrow the money."

Joyce admits she was never really a good student, and recalls one particularly humiliating moment when she was in third grade.

> Joyce: "I sat in the front row of the class and Miss Reid was teaching us how to tell time. I had a difficult time learning the concept and instead of being patient with me, she put her hand on top of my head and announced to the class, 'Joyce Cohn, you are so dumb. You will never amount to anything!' "

Joyce remembered that awful moment when she was in the Colorado state senate. A colleague was arguing for more teachers without including the important statement that teachers need to know how to deal with children of all learning capacities.

> Joyce: "That moment from third grade has stayed with me my whole life. Well guess what, Miss Reid, I did amount to something!"

Still, academics took a back seat for Joyce in high school and she often was banished to the hallways for talking too much in class. But she was never in any real trouble and was elected to the student council.

As her 50th high school reunion approached in 2011 Joyce prepared a speech.

> Joyce: "I was prepared but no one asked me to speak!"

Here's part of what Joyce would have said: "Trying to remember each other, which has definitely become more difficult because we've grown white hair, lines on our faces, and tummies, so it's good to have the yearbook to really remember who we are. … We are a very special group of people. We grew up with good values. I tell people I didn't know how poor I was because my mom made lamb chops for dinner. So, when people in Denver ask why is it a big deal going to a high school reunion I answer it is because those memories are part and parcel of the person I've become and the values I share with my children and grandchildren."

After high school graduation, Joyce attended a year of community college in Benton Harbor and then moved to Chicago in hopes of getting her "Mrs. Degree" – landing a husband. She worked at Marshall Field's and other jobs while attending night classes at Northwestern University at the downtown campus. She had more interest in the students than her classes.

"In high school, she was a party girl who liked to have fun and liked the boys," Joyce's childhood friend, Enid Goldstein, said. "Grades were not an issue. If anyone had asked me in high school if Joyce would marry a rabbi and become president of a city council I would have said they were dropping acid."

Jewish girls in Benton Harbor loved visiting Chicago, Enid explained. "Benton Harbor was a small town of mostly Protestants. We were able to get dressed up, like we never would have at home, and go to the big city. It was such an adventure."

After dating a non-Jewish man, to her parents' horror, and working different jobs to support herself as a single woman in Chicago, Joyce first connected with Steve through phone conversations.

Steve was one of the weekend directors at the camp in Oconomowoc and he would drive about 50 miles one way from Madison each weekend. He also was teaching Sunday school in Madison so he would end up making three round trips each weekend to fulfill both jobs. On Mondays, he would speak to Joyce – who worked in the camp's Chicago office – by phone to update their mutual boss about the number of people who came to the camp, often in groups from Chicago. When the work schedule got to be too much for Steve their boss agreed to send Joyce by train from Chicago to Oconomowoc so that Steve could show her how to do the camp job.

Here comes the Hollywood script part of when we first met. Steve drove to the train station in Watertown, near Oconomowoc, to pick up Joyce in December 1964.

Steve: "She got off the train in her gray herringbone suit and I fell in love with her. Love at first sight at 6 in the evening. Before midnight, I asked her to marry me."

Joyce: "Just look at his face. He was, is, drop dead handsome. And Jewish!"

The Jewish part was very important because Joyce had recently ended a relationship with a non-Jewish man that caused her parents much heartburn. At one point her father threatened to drive to Chicago to bring her back to Benton Harbor. They had learned about the relationship from her sister.

Joyce: "Steve solved that problem. I hit the jackpot! What else, he's going to be a rabbi! He was a Super Jew!"

Steve was love-struck and shared the news with his skeptical sister.

"Steve came to our apartment and announced, 'I'm in love!' and I started to laugh," Syril said. "He asked why I was laughing and I told him, 'because he was always in love.' Before he met Joyce he flirted around. The girls adored him and the charisma didn't hurt. So, I laughed. Then he said he was going to marry her and I just said 'okay' but I continued to giggle because I thought she was just one of many."

His sister's reaction didn't deter Steve and he invited Joyce back to Milwaukee for New Year's Eve.

We spoke often by phone, and even though Joyce was now getting paid to visit the camp in Oconomowoc, Steve still made the trip to see her.

However, we hit a blip when Steve promised to come to Chicago for Joyce's birthday in February and then he canceled.

These are the first photographs we exchanged when we started dating. Steve carried the one of Joyce for 50 years in his wallet or displayed it in his office. Joyce initially sent Steve's photo in a letter to her parents to introduce them to her new boyfriend.

Steve: "I'm not sure what I was thinking at the time. I was on cloud nine and then kind of went to cloud four. I was looking at a big commitment in graduate school and wasn't sure about more."

We continued to talk by phone and Joyce was thrilled when Steve invited her to come to Madison for a visit in April.

Joyce: "I called my mom and dad on a Friday night and told them I was going to Madison and I was sure he was going to have a ring. We had a really good time on Friday night, but on Saturday. ..."

Steve broke up with her. At the time he just didn't feel they had a future. Heartbroken, Joyce stayed with his roommates while Steve went to teach Sunday school. She planned to take a train back to Chicago that day but then Joyce got the call that changed both of our lives.

"Joyce was in Madison and I had to make the call," said her sister, Sharon. "It was terrible, just terrible."

Joyce's father had killed himself after an episode of severe depression. Sharon believes the turning point came when she and her husband, Joel, were planning a big wedding in the fall of 1964.

"We moved up the wedding date to November and had a small wedding," she recalled. "My father got caught up in the hoopla and he just got worse and worse. I think of the three of us my sister had the hardest time with our father's death. She was the closest to him."

Jack, a sophomore at the University of Michigan, also got the news by phone about his father's death.

"I hitch-hiked from school to Benton Harbor," he said. "It was a Sunday and it was a rough day. I just got on the road and a couple of people picked me up."

Joyce was in shock and Steve's roommates called him at the temple where he was teaching religious school; he immediately headed back to the apartment to pick up Joyce. On the drive to Benton Harbor, we stopped in Milwaukee to switch cars. Steve's sister, Syril, said she would go with us and we all headed to the funeral.

This was the first time Steve and Syril had met anyone in Joyce's family.

"On the way back to Benton Harbor I think we drove through a tornado," Syril recalled. "Of course we were young and foolish and we had Joyce sitting in the middle and it was awful for her. We had planned to stay in a hotel but her mother wouldn't allow it. I got to share a bed with Joyce's sister, who had been recently married, and I had never met any of these folks before and it was very difficult."

After the funeral on the trip back to Milwaukee, Steve was deep in thought about the last few days and told Syril he was still unsure about his future with Joyce.

"I said she's bright, she's beautiful and I didn't say much more," Syril said.

> Steve: "I was rethinking everything and instead of turning away I was coming closer to realizing what I would have lost."

We spoke a lot by phone the following month. And then Steve called Joyce's mother and asked for her daughter's hand in marriage. Joyce was still in the dark but Steve told his parents so that they could plan a surprise engagement party when Joyce came to visit.

Joyce thought she was going to Milwaukee just for Friday services with Steve and his family.

Steve's parents drove their car to temple and we went separately in Steve's Chevy Corvair. That car had the engine in the rear, which was perfect for Steve's surprise. After services, Steve drove the lakeshore and then pretended to have engine trouble and stopped. He went to the rear and opened the hood.

Steve: "I came back to Joyce and said, 'Look what I found in the engine,' and I was holding my mother's diamond ring that she gave me and we used it as our engagement ring."

The next night Joyce's mother, sister, and brother-in-law joined Steve's family at the engagement party in Milwaukee.

Steve: "I finally realized what a mistake I was going to make."

Joyce: "I've always said he felt sorry for me; therefore, he married me."

As is tradition in a Jewish family we were still in mourning over the passing of Joyce's father.

Initially, we planned to marry in June 1966 but after Steve attended summer school in Cincinnati in 1965 and lived with a bunch of guys in a dormitory, he was ready for Joyce to join him in an apartment.

We got married on December 26, 1965 and Joyce wore her sister's wedding gown.

Joyce: "We were so young, 22 and 21. I didn't care about my own gown. It didn't bother me because she had a

Our wedding day was a joyous occasion but missing from the family portrait was Joyce's father, Bill Cohn, (facing page, pictured in the family clothing shop with a new heater). Gathering with us on Dec. 26, 1965 was Joyce's sister, Sharon, (front left) and Steve's sister, Syril (front right), Joyce's brother, Jack (top left), her mother, Beverly and Steve's parents, Miriam and Milton Foster.

beautiful gown and it was the best my mom could do. It was a lovely wedding but there was no music because my father had passed away and we were still grieving. We had a nice dinner. His parents had a nice rehearsal dinner on Christmas Day. We were lucky to find a place."

After the wedding at the synagogue, we headed to our reception but nobody greeted us when we arrived.

Steve: "The Green Bay Packers were playing the Baltimore Colts for the championship game. Everyone was gathered around the television in the lobby and focused on the game."

Joyce: "Not one person saw us walk in or even turned around."

Of course, we're also Packers fans – well, Steve has been since birth and Joyce learned to love the team – so we understood the game was more important than our arrival as a married couple.

While this chapter has a happy ending with our marriage, little did we know that the illness that struck Joyce's father also would be a challenge for our daughter.

We also had no clue about the challenges we would face as newlyweds before we planted new roots in Denver that would grow deep and spread wide for more than 40 years.

2

Rabbinical School and Early Clergy Life

The challenges and joys

Student clergy couples starting out often face conflicts where one person is immersed in studies – or a new congregation - while the spouse is looking for a passion. At the time, both of us may not have realized that conflict was there because honestly, we were living day-to-day, inching closer to the time when Steve would graduate and land his first assignment.

The lesson, looking back, is as a couple you can weather the challenges. We did. And what we learned from those experiences we used as older adults – whether counseling engaged couples, married couples or helping resettle immigrant Jewish couples in their new homeland.

Shortly after our wedding we headed to Cincinnati, where Steve studied to be a rabbi and Joyce worked as a headhunter in employment services to help pay the bills. We were living in a small apartment and getting used to a new city.

While Steve was busy with his studies, Joyce got to know the other students' wives and felt somewhat lost. Most of the women had graduated from college and had teaching degrees.

> Joyce: "I felt very inadequate during that time in my life. Since I worked in employment recruiting I chose to get back in the field. I worked on commission for Snelling and Snelling and actually earned more than most of the wives who had college degrees."

All of the student rabbis had assignments at synagogues that had smaller congregations and didn't have full-time rabbis. The students usually spent a short time at several synagogues. But Steve had a unique situation because he stayed with the same synagogue in Union City, Tennessee for three years.

Once or twice a month we'd drive to the airport together and Steve would board a plane for Union City, where he would spend the weekend. But during High Holy weeks the members of that temple usually traveled to Memphis so that allowed Steve to be available for another assignment.

During the High Holy Days from 1967 to 1969, Steve traveled to Casper, Wyoming, which eventually would help lead us to Denver.

Joyce later wrote how she and other students' wives felt very lonely when their husbands were on the out-of-town assignments, especially during the High Holy Days. "It was a good experience for the men – a lonely one for the women. For one

In August 1966, we took a belated honeymoon and break from Steve's graduate studies and our jobs in Cincinnati to visit Florida and Nassau in the Bahamas.

month, the men locked themselves into their studies to prepare the sermons and then, off to their weekend destination."

Steve also worked as a tutor and for three years owned a day camp in Cincinnati. His family helped us financially with about $100 a month but otherwise we paid the bills ourselves.

Our jobs allowed us to keep on top of our bills. When we left graduate school we left with a much smaller debt than many of the other classmates and we were able to pay that debt pretty quickly. In contrast, it took years for many of Steve's classmates to pay off their school debt.

During Steve's time in rabbinical school Joyce still was emotionally rocked by her father's death. She couldn't help but think back to him making breakfast for her and her siblings when they were kids. She remembered him saying she was the prettiest girl in the room when she lost a high-school beauty pageant. She remembered him offering to drop everything and drive 90 miles to Chicago to pick her up and bring her home when she was lonely and living on her own in the big city.

She admired his creative mind. He met with Sammy Davis Jr. to get the actor to be the face of a local wine company and he had a hula hoop made into an industrial size and pitched the novelty to the Notre Dame athletic department.

Each creative idea frizzled and frazzled her mother, who became a target of Joyce's grief after her father's death.

> Joyce: "I blamed my mother. My mother would yell at him all of the time. You don't yell at someone who is mentally ill, but she didn't know. She was working hard to make sure we had food on our table and the store was running well. They had creditors on their backs all the time."

That animosity quickly faded and her mother ended up moving to Denver a few years after we arrived in 1970. Crime in Benton Harbor was becoming an issue. Sharon recalled how Joyce's mother had to install an alarm system in the shop and once she triggered the alarm during an attempted robbery. The robbers made her lie on the floor while they ransacked the store.

"Our mother was gutsy and lifted herself off the floor high enough to hit and trigger the alarm that brought police," Sharon said.

As newlyweds in Cincinnati, we had to get used to living with each other and how our childhood influenced us as adults. This was a lesson Steve would later use when he counseled young couples as a rabbi.

For example, his father never took part in household duties like washing dishes. He'd come home from work the same time every weekday, sit in the living room, read the newspaper and get up when he was called to supper. A family joke is that his father didn't know the home had a kitchen because he never walked in there.

For Joyce, her father did more domestic tasks because they had the shop. Her mother was a good cook but he got the kids up and to school most days. Couples need to adjust to these differences and Steve learned quickly he was expected to help with the dishes and other duties.

> Steve: "I'm always telling married couples the roles people play in a marriage are based upon the roles that your parents played when you were growing up."

And because those roles are different, couples need to adjust and that's not always easy.

Young couples also may face the challenges of being young parents.

> Joyce: "We got married in 1965 and two and half years later I was pregnant with David. And I was suddenly on unemployment. They fired me because I was pregnant. You could be fired then for being pregnant. I collected $50 a week in unemployment but according to unemployment rules I still had to look for a job, even though no one would ever hire a pregnant woman at that time."

> Steve: "Denying pregnant woman work is another civil rights issue."

After David's birth, Steve faced two more years of graduate school and working while Joyce stayed home and focused on motherhood.

> Steve: "I did the night feedings for all of our three kids and a lot of men of my generation didn't do that. They thought it was the woman's job."

But Joyce was on her own when Steve needed to travel for his synagogue duties. When Steve went to Casper he had to change planes at the former Stapleton International Airport in Denver.

> Steve: "I would come for two weeks and I fell in love with the area. The year I was ordained, 1970, Rabbi Earl Stone was the senior rabbi at Temple Emanuel in Denver and he was looking for an assistant. Stuart Geller, a classmate who was from Denver, said I would be perfect for Stone. ... There were 28 people in my class and 24 wanted that job. There were two of us who were invited

When Steve arrived at Temple Emanuel in Denver in 1970 he was thrilled to inherit a desk used by a rabbi from his childhood. Former Denver Rabbi Herbert Friedman served at Temple Emanuel before moving to Milwaukee when Steve was about 10. He was well known for being outspoken on social justice issues.

for a second interview. I was one of them and I got the job. I was thrilled. I got the plum job."

Ernie Abramson, board president of Temple Emanuel at the time, came to the interview with Rabbi Stone. Joyce credits herself for Steve landing the job because Ernie invited her and 16-month-old David for a hot dog in the student cafeteria.

Joyce: "Ernie and I had a great visit. Years later he told me Steve got the job because of me!"

Steve: "True, Ernie thought Joyce was wonderful."

Rabbi Stone was 56 when he offered Steve the job. He came to Denver from Cleveland in 1956 with the goal of helping heal a rift in the Jewish community. In Denver and nationally there was a split among Jews about the establishment of Israel. The division was about whether Jews should be seen as a people – therefore sanctioning the establishment of the state of Israel – or whether Judaism should be seen solely as a religion.

In 1970, Temple Emanuel had a new goal of attracting more young couples and Rabbi Stone wanted an assistant who could help make that happen. Board members also were hoping that the new assistant would stay for several years and possibly step in as senior rabbi when Rabbi Stone retired.

We liked the idea of settling in to one congregation, because most assistant rabbis serve at temples for three years and then move on.

Joyce was thrilled to be moving to Denver's largest synagogue, because she did not want to be the rabbi's wife in a small congregation in a small town.

> Joyce: "I grew up in a small town and I could see what they did to rabbis and their spouses... everyone was always talking about the rabbi or the spouse. I told Steve, 'I'm happy to be married to you and be a rebbetzin, but boy, you better choose a big city.' I was never going to go back to that because as a kid I remember the comments I heard – not from my parents because they never talked about the rabbis – but their friends. And it was not pleasant."

Temple Emanuel, the largest Jewish congregation between Kansas City and the West Coast, also is the oldest Jewish congregation in the state of Colorado and was founded in 1874.

The temple had about 900 families when Steve began his job on July 1, 1970. By the time he retired on May 22, 2010 the number had grown to more than 2,200 families.

When we arrived in Denver with our 22-month-old son, David, and 17-day-old son, Danny, we were young clergy diving into a new congregation.

Rabbi Friedman still played a role in Steve's life because Steve inherited the desk Friedman used when he was in Denver. From behind that desk Steve crafted sermons that would touch upon such subjects as school busing, the Vietnam War, the impact of drugs on minorities, the Rocky Flats nuclear plant near Boulder, and ongoing civil rights issues.

Throughout the 40 years, he would take a leadership role in calling for gay rights, standing up to Ku Klux Klan marchers, and returning his beloved Boy Scout medals when the organization enacted anti-gay policies. He served as a member of the Colorado Civil Rights Commission for 12 years and as its chair for four years.

Those sermons began to mold his role as the "voice of the Jewish community" for the next four decades, not just because Temple Emanuel was the largest synagogue in the region but also because Steve never hesitated to address social justice issues.

> Steve: "I believe that there is room enough for politics and for religion and they both have to meet somewhere in the common place. The political people, according to our system of government, have to at least listen to the religious voice, even though the religious voice is going to be varied and difficult."

While Steve settled into his new role, Joyce felt somewhat isolated with a toddler and baby in a new community. Other clergy wives can likely relate to this.

As a young mother, Joyce jotted down her feelings on a yellow note pad.

"The baby was all of 17 days old, his brother all of 22 months, and their father was at the temple waiting for the phone to ring," Joyce wrote. "I was feeding two babies, changing two sets of diapers and answering door bells from neighbors. Our furniture didn't arrive on time; I didn't know where to secure sitters; and I was already answering wedding and bar mitzvah invitations!"

She especially felt the loneliness during the High Holidays.

"Now that we finally made the big time [in Denver] I was truly looking forward to festive holiday seasons – boy, was I wrong," Joyce wrote. "You see, these are his busiest times. Back to the study for a month of sermon writing, mixed in of course with the opening of the religious school; crisis counseling; a few funerals; and whatever else.

"Now, I plan a real gedempte meal [braised chicken or brisket] and that goes over like a lead matzo ball! When we have to eat at 4:30 p.m. and no one is hungry and he doesn't want to eat much before preaching. Well, it just takes the fun out of cooking."

Steve knew he would have a different style than his boss, Rabbi Stone, who as we mentioned was brought to Denver to help heal the Jewish community and did not like to make waves. He was very good with the life cycle events of bar mitzvahs, weddings, and funerals but shied away from social justice issues.

Our family in 1975: oldest son David (far left), daughter, Debbie and Danny (sporting the bow tie).

In contrast, Steve was hired as the assistant in a time the board wanted to attract younger couples and during a time of great civil unrest.

Steve: "To me, religion is not just about what the prayer book says. To me, religion is about what I think God demands of us in terms of how we ought to be there and to make what God wants this world to be. So, when people say, 'Stick to religion,' I do. These are the issues that are important to me. Some people say, 'Talk about God'; I do because this is what I think God wants… I think religion is about how we function in the world and how we make a difference to bring about in religious terms God's kingdom on earth. God's kingdom on earth will be when people live in peace and people understand each other. And if we can help government to bring that day closer, that's our job."

While Steve was making his mark, Joyce was being directed by Judy Stone on her role as a rabbi's wife at Temple Emanuel. She told Joyce not to pick and choose which events to attend. If she were going to accept one invitation, she should accept them all. And for the next 40 years, that's exactly what Joyce did.

Joyce: "I chose afternoon bar/bat mitzvahs and didn't attend mornings until my children were much older."

She didn't do it just because that was what was expected of her at the time.

Joyce: "I chose to attend a lot of the functions so I could see Steve. And as a bonus, people would see me and it was not a bad thing. I was always pretty extroverted. I always liked people."

But she was always careful about how she dressed, because clergy spouses are on display.

Joyce: "When you dress too well, you'll hear: 'Why does he need a salary increase? They look like they're doing well enough.' And when you dress a little dowdy one hears: 'She really has no taste.' Once during rabbinical school, a professor's wife said: 'Stay away from wearing a red dress – it looks a little too flashy!' "

But Joyce ignored that advice.

Joyce: "I love red and wore it all the time!"

Joyce's bright red fingernail polish also has been her signature look for more than 40 years.

"One of my jobs when I worked for Joyce when she was on the city council was doing her schedule," Sharon Elfenbein recalled. "There was only one thing I could never reschedule: her nail appointment."

Joyce may have ignored some fashion advice but she learned to cultivate relationships as a young rabbi's wife. By the time Steve was promoted to senior rabbi, Joyce's years of relationship-building helped the congregation embrace them.

> Steve: "The spouses of clergy don't have to be there all of the time but I do think you have to be present some time. People like to look around and see you there. I don't think that is any different in a church or synagogue. Sunday morning at a church I think people want to see the minister and the minister's spouse engaging with people. Because that's what it is all about: creating a community. And Joyce helped create a community."

Perhaps we could have set limits on always being available – sometimes at the cost to our own family – but we took it seriously and committed to our jobs of being on call 24/7. Steve even left our family vacations when necessary to fly home for funerals or other emergencies.

Steve and Natalie Goldman experienced our hectic schedules firsthand while we were on trips together or having meals at a restaurant.

"It was hard to find time to do things together because they were so busy," Natalie recalled. "We'd be out to dinner together and someone would recognize them and want to visit.

… They lived in a glass house and their jobs were 24 hours a day. Because I saw that firsthand, I said I didn't want my children to be a rabbi."

This dedication was important for Steve to grow the congregation, including attracting more young couples. Rabbi Stone asked Steve, as an assistant rabbi, to expand a group called the Mr. and Mrs. Club, patterned after a similar group Rabbi Stone started in Cleveland.

The idea was to have couples socialize and get to know each other. When Steve arrived, there were a handful of couples in the club. Rabbi Stone initially just wanted members of temple to participate but Steve pushed to expand it to nonmembers.

> Steve: "Eventually we had 120 couples in the club and many ended up joining temple."

> Joyce: "The couples got to know each other and know Steve and me and that made them want to be part of temple."

Steve and Natalie Goldman moved to Denver in 1971 and said the Mr. and Mrs. Club helped them settle in their new city.

"We have friends all over the country and the friendships began in the Mr. and Mrs. Club," Natalie said. "It really helped us get to know other Jewish couples in Denver and made us feel part of the community."

Also related to marriage, when Steve was still the assistant rabbi we were invited to a weekend for Jewish Marriage Encounter. We had never heard of the group but with three small children at home we thought it sounded like a good way to get away and learn something.

The encounter was a weekend at a local inexpensive hotel,

where couples could get away from any distractions and focus on their marriages. We were excited to attend because many of the Mr. and Mrs. Club members from our temple also were participating.

We were able to go because Joyce's mother spent the weekend at our house with the live-in student who helped with our three children.

> Joyce: "The goal of marriage encounter was to make marriages stronger through dialogue in a nonjudgmental environment. No one but the presenters shared anything personal. We found the weekend to be one of renewal and discovery. The presenters consisted of a rabbinic couple and three lay couples who followed an outline sharing their personal stories. We loved this concept."

The lead couples wrote out the agenda for the weekend, which included guides to the participating couples on how to communicate.

One lead couple would get in front of an audience of about 20 couples and tell their story, followed by the rabbinic couples. Then the couples in the audience would go back to their rooms and privately open up to each other and also take the lessons home.

> Joyce: "You cannot judge each other; these are feelings and not thoughts. And you cannot judge someone else's feelings; it's their feelings to own."

> Steve: "I still use some of that material when I do premarital stuff. I talk about the difference between thoughts and feelings and how do you deal with feelings. You know,

when you say to someone, 'You have nice blue eyes,' it's not a feeling, it's a thought. But if I said, 'I appreciate your blue eyes,' that is my feelings. So there are differences between thoughts and feelings and that all had to be modeled for the couples."

We were asked to our first encounter to be trained for future presentations. They covered our costs of two nights in the hotel, three meals a day and snacks.

Joyce: "We had been invited by two 'seasoned' rabbinical presenting couples to think about becoming a presenting couple. We were flattered and overwhelmed by the eventual commitment that we had made. Rabbi and Mrs. Neil Brief and Rabbi and Mrs. Murray Blackman trained us. Then we traveled all over the country to present. We arrived on Fridays in time for Shabbat and left on Monday."

We conducted about three marriage encounter events a year.

Steve: "We went to Chicago, New Orleans, Detroit, Dallas... we went to a lot of places that we were invited to and we would meet other couples. There weren't that many rabbis throughout the country who were doing it, so we were sort of on the circuit."

Joyce: "The only problem was the encounters took place in hotels near airports and there was no time to see anything except the inside of our meeting rooms."

We met some lovely people. Many couples who participated locally ended up becoming members of Temple Emanuel.

Shwayder camp became a big part of our family from the time we arrived in Denver. Our children, David (left raising his hand), Danny (right of Steve) and Debbie (not pictured) attended the camp, we participated in activities, and Steve raised money to expand the camp located in the mountains west of Denver. As adults, David and Danny continue to fundraise for the camp where their children attend activities.

In Denver, we presented with our dear friends Marcia and Ken Light; Myrna and Bob Siegel; and Anne and Howie Jacobs.

> Joyce: "I can't say that Steve and I dialogued daily as we counseled, but it was a special time for us. We encouraged my sister, Sharon, and her husband, Joel, to try a group in Chicago. They loved the many new friends they made and still see them today."

We conducted the presentations for about five years and stopped for a couple of reasons. It was very time-consuming and kind of ran its course for us. And we lost one of the presenting couples in 1985 when Howie died unexpectedly at age 51 and left Anne a young widow.

> Joyce: "We were inspired by them because of their commitment to each other and their writings were spectacular."

> Steve: "Their love for each other was just so absolutely beautiful."

Besides our work with married couples, another area that helped grow the congregation was starting a Reform preschool at temple. Our sons were too young for school when we arrived in Denver in the summer of 1970 but the temple's mountain Shwayder Camp directors, Mort and Judy Hoffman, were teachers. Judy approached Steve about starting the preschool.

> Steve: "So, I went to Rabbi Stone and he said, 'Alright, but you have to go to the board.' So, I went to the board and said, 'Here is what I would like to do. We want to start a preschool, one class with 12 children, and I need $100 for toys and to paint the walls.' Their reaction was, Oh, well that is a lot of money and let's not spend money we don't have to spend. But I promised them that I would never come back for more money and in the end I didn't. It was $100 on the part of the board and now there are more than 350 children and it provides a sizeable income for the synagogue."

Steve had the preschool open by January 1971.

Judy served as the preschool's first director and was wonderful not only with providing good programs for the students but also testing kids for learning disabilities.

Carol Boigon, who would become a close political adviser later for Joyce, recalls how that preschool helped during a family crisis. Carol and her husband, Howard, moved to Denver with their baby and a 3-year-old foster daughter who they suspected had been abused and had emotional issues.

They settled in a nice Denver neighborhood and a neighbor suggested a nearby preschool for the girl but the preschool turned them down.

"Even though she was only 25 pounds and 3 years old, they said they didn't want her," Boigon recalled. "I was heartbroken and far from home and I didn't know what to do. So, being a Jewish woman I looked for help from the Jewish community."

Boigon opened the phone book and the first temple listed was Temple Emanuel.

"I called and got a secretary and my story came tumbling out. The receptionist said, 'You should speak to Rabbi Steve; he started our preschool,' " Boigon said. "He calmed me down and said of course we could come to the school and they would work through any issues. I knew from that minute that he was my friend. So, of course, when many years later Joyce asked for my help on her city council campaign, my answer was, 'Anything you want.' "

Because of the popularity of the preschool, the parents later wanted a kindergarten at temple and eventually a full-time religious day school. Our vision was to have kindergarten through sixth grade to begin. But this idea caused a rift on a couple of fronts.

The Denver Public Schools had recently started court-mandated busing to integrate the schools. Many members of our congregation pushed for busing and saw us opening a religious day school at temple as an affront. A group of about 50 members circulated a petition and threatened to leave temple if the school opened.

So we knew after the board accepted the petition that the school would have to be separate from the synagogue. The director of the Allied Jewish Federation asked us to meet with the orthodox day school in Denver before we moved forward with our plans. The federation got involved because it helps fund Jewish day schools.

The orthodox day school wasn't thrilled with our plans because it feared it would lose enrollment when we opened a new school. At the time, there were few Reform day schools around the country.

> Steve: "We sat down with the orthodox school leaders and the meeting started with the principal of the school saying they were prepared to give 'a watered-down program to the watered-down Jews.' So we, the watered-down Jews, got up from the table and walked away still determined to open the new school."

Independent of their synagogues, Steve was joined by three liberal rabbis in supporting the new school: Rabbi Raymond Zwerin of Temple Sinai, Rabbi Bernard Eisenman of Congregation Rodef Shalom, and Rabbi Harold Krantzler of Temple Micah helped recruit students.

Our family in 1983: David (far left), Debbie and Danny.

The Theodor Herzl Jewish Day School (Herzl) opened in 1975 with 14 students in grades 1-5. In 1979, the Rocky Mountain Hebrew Academy was established with 10 students in grades 9-12. In 1998, the two school boards voted to merge the schools into one and established the Denver Campus for Jewish Education, which is now called the Denver Jewish Day School for kindergarten through 12th grade students. It has more than 340 students.

Our three children went through sixth grade at Herzl and still have friendships with many of their former classmates.

The lesson is if your community has a need, you need to find a way to fulfill it even if others – including members of your congregation – disagree.

Over the years, Steve helped raise a significant amount of money to support programs for Sunday school students to take trips to New York, Cincinnati, and Israel to learn about leadership and Judaism.

Steve received an unexpected donation that helped fund those trips and other temple needs. Francis Goldsmith was not a member of temple but he was impressed with a eulogy Steve had given at his longtime friend's funeral. Goldsmith's friend, a woman, had fled from Germany to Shanghai before World War II because of the Nazis.

When Steve did the eulogy he spoke about how there were many different kinds of survivors of the Holocaust, including those who survived the death camps and those who had no choice but to flee Germany and start new lives – often in a foreign country and having to learn a new language.

When Francis Goldsmith died, his attorney called Steve and asked him if he would perform the man's funeral service even though Goldsmith was not a member of temple. When Steve said yes, the attorney surprised Steve and said Goldsmith had stipulated in his will that if Steve did his funeral service he would bequeath $800,000 to the temple. Goldsmith had no family.

Steve used that money to help high school students fund their Israel Study Tour, buy books and supplies for the temple's library, fund needs at Shwayder Camp, and to help pay for trips for 9th graders to visit the Hebrew college in Cincinnati and 10th graders to visit different neighborhoods in New York City, which is called the Jewish Roots Mission.

Clergy never know how people will respond to a kindness offered to a stranger. If Steve had said no to the man's funeral service, the temple and its young members would not have benefited from the generous donation.

It is important to continue to grow education opportunities for our young congregation members, and for us the religious day school was a major step.

Our congregation's desire to have a day school has benefited generations of Jewish families in Denver. But we didn't know that when we began with only 14 students. We took the risk and it has benefited our community.

Years before we saw the day school grow, we worked to settle in Denver. Our lives took some unexpected turns when Joyce's mother decided to move to Denver and Joyce later was offered a job at Jewish Family Service.

And little did we know then that 20 years after we arrived in Denver one of us would help shape the future of our new city as an elected official.

3

Interfaith Marriage and a Rabbi's Working Wife

Steve's Stepping Stones program

and Joyce's new careers

Every clergy – whether a rabbi or a minister – often has certain subjects or causes he or she feels a particular passion for. They don't take away from daily duties and often they provide a valuable service to the community.

In 1977, we were in a regular routine, with Steve a busy assistant rabbi and Joyce taking care of our children. They included our daughter, Debbie, who was three years old. By this time Joyce's mother had moved to Denver, leaving her store in

Benton Harbor in the hands of a trusted employee. She was widowed in 1965 and wanted to start over in a new city. She became an invaluable back-up babysitter and established new friendships in Denver.

That year, two things changed our routines: Steve went to graduate school and Joyce began work at Jewish Family Service.

Steve attended classes at the Iliff School of Theology part-time for his doctorate in pastoral counseling. He had a deep interest in the issues of conversion to Judaism and intermarriage, and they would become the topics of his doctoral project several years later. He was awarded his doctorate from Iliff in 1985 and also earned a Doctor of Divinity degree from Hebrew Union College-Jewish Institute of Religion in Cincinnati in 1995.

It was a natural fit for Steve to choose intermarriage as his doctoral theme at Iliff. His interest in intermarriage runs deep because statistically the majority of Jews who marry non-Jews who do not convert end up raising their children as non-Jews.

Steve: "Demographically, that is a disaster for the Jewish community."

In 1981, the same year Steve became senior rabbi at Temple Emanuel, he was chosen as the National Rabbinic Chair for the Outreach Commission, which was a national movement to address all of the issues surrounding intermarriage.

Steve: "Our task nationally was to develop programs to integrate interfaith couples into congregational life. We reached out to the non-Jewish spouse and at least offered the opportunity, if they wanted to think about conversion. We also reached out to the parents of interfaith couples, Jewish and

52

Gentile, because there is a lot of pain involved in interfaith marriages. In addition, we began working to develop programs for the children of the interfaith couples."

Steve was traveling all over the country to work with rabbis and lay people. The lay person in charge was David Belin, an attorney from Des Moines. Belin was well known for having served on the Warren Commission and writing the report that Lee Harvey Oswald acted alone in the assassination of President John F. Kennedy.

Steve worked on the Outreach Commission for 15 years and during that time started a Denver area program, which he called "Stepping Stones to a Jewish Me." He expanded the programs we had developed in the Outreach Commission for children. Saundra Heller was the first director of Stepping Stones.

Steve and Saundra created a Sunday afternoon Stepping Stones program for interfaith families throughout the metro Denver area that was free. Regular Sunday school teachers provided the education for the program, which meant we had to raise money to pay the teachers.

The first year about 60 children attended and attendance grew as more interfaith couples heard about the program.

Steve: "Stepping Stones to a Jewish Me was a program to reach out to those couples who intermarried and said they were going to raise their children in 'both faiths' and then let them choose when they are older. That's a recipe for disaster because their kids are going to be raised in confusion. They are not going to be raised with a sense of identity. So we started this program to give kids of interfaith families and their parents an idea of what it would mean

53

to be Jewish and 70 percent of the parents who went through the program decided to raise their children as Jews."

The program included such topics as the confusion of children who celebrate both Christmas and Hanukah and Easter and Passover.

Over the years our family's involvement in Stepping Stones also grew because when Debbie was an adult she became a teacher in the program and later its educational director.

> Joyce: "And many years later we still run into people who tell us that Debbie was very welcoming and helped their family member with their Jewish education."

Stepping Stones received press coverage and a few other out-of-state temples started similar programs with it as the blueprint. Shortly before Steve retired, a Jewish group headed by a millionaire businessman from Atlanta reached out to Steve with interest in expanding Stepping Stones nationally.

> Steve: "We set up our goals and they agreed with them and they gave us money to do certain things. Then all of a sudden they decided our program wasn't big enough to replicate in other places. Three of us even went to Atlanta to meet with them and one guy said I hit a home run. Eighteen months later, it was strike three and we were out."

Janet Bronitsky, executive director of Temple Emanuel, worked with Steve on Stepping Stones. While the program is no longer active, she said the temple still reaches out to non-Jewish family members.

"It was a really important concept and it still is – to reach out and let the community know we care about families that are interfaith and how they choose to raise their children," she said.

It was a blow for Steve when the program didn't go national because he saw directing Stepping Stones as a full-time job after he retired from the temple.

Steve: "There's no question intermarriage is more acceptable now than to our generation, but what is going to happen to us as a people? Here is an example. I had a funeral and the man who died had three daughters. One is married to a Jew and they raised their children Jewish. The other two married outside the faith and their children are not Jewish. That example is why it is a disaster for us."

While Steve has strong opinions on intermarriage, we never gave our children a hard time about dating non-Jews.

"I recently told this story to a buddy of mine whose daughter is dating someone he didn't like," our son, David, recalled. "I said let me tell you about my parents. They saw me and Danny dating many women over the years and some more serious than others and they were never anything but welcoming. Many of those women were not Jewish and my parents did not judge them or question us."

David suspects we may have had private discussions about the women not being Jewish but we never brought that up with our sons. We also didn't pressure Debbie to find a Jewish mate.

We accepted the people they dated because we believed their strong faith would eventually lead them to partners with the same beliefs, and that is what happened.

We were thrilled when our daughter-in-law, Becky, converted before she married Danny and both David and Debbie married Jewish mates. We're still close to our former son-in-law, Matt Leebove, who also has remained friends with Debbie.

When Becky and Danny started dating it wasn't serious and they had a few breakups before it became serious. Becky wasn't brought up in a religious home but she had an uncle who converted after he married a Jewish woman. Danny brought Becky to our Shabbat dinners and High Holidays and she had Jewish friends so she was familiar with Judaism.

"Once we started getting serious – finally – it was something I definitely needed to consider," Becky recalled of her conversion. "For me, I had no attachment to a religion and my parents were both very open-minded. Danny's family always made it very easy for me. Being around his family and services helped me know for certain that this was something I could see myself becoming and raising my children."

Becky, who teaches secular classes at an orthodox Jewish day school, Denver Academy of Torah, has friends who raise their children in two religions.

"I do see how that would be confusing," she said. "My kids really don't know my side of the family well just because they are in Wisconsin and Danny's family is down the block. They know they are Jewish and they don't think they are anything but Jewish."

Steve: "And Becky to us is Jewish."

Four years before Steve got involved in the Outreach Commission, Joyce unexpectedly was recruited by Jewish Family Service for a part-time job in 1977. She wasn't looking for work but they asked her to take a job as the employment director.

JFS provides a number of services for the Jewish community and community at-large, from employment to housing to helping senior citizens.

Steve's salary as an assistant rabbi met our needs as a young family but we knew extra income would be nice because we had tuition for our three children to attend day school. Joyce worked with JFS until 1993, when she was elected to the Denver City Council, and the income also helped pay their college tuitions.

Joyce helped clients fill out applications and dress properly for interviews, and then she took them to the job interviews. That role became even more significant when Colorado welcomed a large number of Russian Jews who were fleeing the Soviet Union in the late 1970s and 1980s.

Many people don't know that Lillian Hoffman, who was born in Denver in 1913, was a leader of the effort to allow Soviet Jews to emigrate to Israel and the United States. She was married to Harry Hoffman, who at the time ran the largest liquor store west of the Mississippi: Hoffman Liquors, in Denver.

Lillian was the longtime chair of the Colorado Committee of Concern for Soviet Jewry (CCCSJ). In 1972, she fought for the passage of the Jackson-Vanik amendment, which threatened U.S. trade sanctions until Soviet Jews were allowed to leave the country.

She traveled to Russia and met with "Refuseniks," a term that referred to the Soviet Jews who were denied permission to leave the country. Rabbi Raymond Zerwin of Temple Sinai in Denver worked closely with Lillian and others to pressure the Soviet government to allow Jews to leave.

Wellington and Wilma Webb, activists in the black community who served in the Colorado legislature and later as Denver's mayor and first lady, remember coming to Temple Emanuel, where we held a protest aimed at forcing the Soviet government to allow Jews to leave the country. The Webbs were members of the America-Israel Friendship League and we had forged a friendship over the years, including inviting them to the temple for a Seder.

"I think we were the only African-Americans at the temple, but we wanted to show our support by protesting the treatment of Soviet Jews," Wellington recalled. "The rallying cry Steve and others made was, 'Let my people go!'"

Through 1991, more than two million Soviet Jews left Russia. Israel wanted the majority of the Soviet Jews to settle there and it became a debate within the Jewish community whether they should have the freedom to choose where they settled.

About a million relocated to Israel and about the same number came to the United States with help from the Hebrew Immigrant Aid Society.

While the Soviet Jews were thrilled to leave Russia, there were cultural differences, and organizations like JFS were very important in helping bridge those differences. There also were sacrifices once they got here. Some Soviet Jews who were doctors or scientists in Russia had to take jobs below their skills here.

Joyce: "I think the most important thing we did through Jewish Family Service and the synagogues was to try to match people up with volunteer host families. The host family would bring the new family to their synagogue and help them with such things as finding furniture, getting to know the city, and learning where the grocery stores are."

Joyce also got a grant from the City and County of Denver for JFS to teach "English as a Second Language" classes for the relocated Jews in Denver.

> Joyce: "I even got a grant where they were getting paid to learn English for nine months. … They all had incentive. Their incentive was survival. Look, they were survivors. These people got out of Russia and they were no longer going to be passive people. I mean, that's who they are and some were very outspoken. They didn't want to settle for a crummy janitorial job if they had been an electrician."

> Steve: "That's why I make this joke: Joyce was so good at her job that there was a plumber in Russia who became a brain surgeon in the United States."

Yana Vishnitsky came to Colorado from the Soviet Union in 1978 and became one of Joyce's good friends. Yana spoke fluent English, was hired by JFS and now serves as its president and CEO.

"First of all, Joyce is the kindest person I have ever met," Vishnitsky said. "She has an incredible ability to connect with a person and connect people together. We witnessed a lot of magic and lives saved at JFS."

Joyce's work at JFS extended from helping the Soviet Jews resettle to helping other clients from throughout the Denver area. She remembers one man, a Denver native who felt abandoned by his family and found himself jobless and homeless. She asked him to compile a list of services for the homeless, which she distributed to all of the synagogues, and in turn she bought him a suit for a job interview.

> Steve: "On a day-to-day basis Joyce was always there to make sure that people got served and it wasn't always with the idea that she was going to get accolades – because in most cases she didn't. She got a thank you and that was enough for her."

Now that we were a two-job family we made sure we had the same days off so we could still spend time together. We both had Mondays off and with the kids in school we could go cross-country skiing or do another activity before we had to pick the kids up from school.

Clergy and political couples sometimes lose themselves in their jobs because they don't spend enough time together. We had to make our time together a priority, even though there wasn't much of it.

But we did get some flak for Joyce taking the job.

> Steve: "When Joyce first went to work I was over at Rose Hospital one day and a doctor, who shall remain nameless, saw me in the parking lot and said, 'Ah, rabbi, I heard your wife went to work. What's the matter? Are you not making enough money?' It was none of his business but in those days he thought it was his business."

Joyce still attended the majority of life-cycle events at the synagogue and we all celebrated when Steve was named the senior rabbi in 1981. His 11 years of hard work as the assistant made the appointment even sweeter, but with the promotion came more expectations from us and others.

We still maintained our commitment to the temple and Steve's voice became even stronger on civil rights issues. Once again Iliff School of Theology played an integral role in our lives.

Steve's work on his doctorate was spread out for a number of years because he took classes part-time. He also built up credits toward his doctorate by taking a two-week intensive class on sexuality and the church, which ran for five days. At the time, Steve didn't know the class was going to focus on the gay community and the Methodist Church, which was going through turmoil in the early 1980s concerning gay men and lesbians being members of the clergy.

One of his classmates was Charlie Arehart, a minister of the Metropolitan Community Church in Denver, which was a church for gay men and women. For Steve, who grew up in the 1940s and 1950s, it was eye-opening to know Charlie, who was gay, and learn more in the class about the gay and lesbian community.

> Steve: "I came to see Charlie not as gay but as a person first and his sexuality was just part of who he is. I understood that his sexuality was not a matter of choice and that was an earth-shattering moment for me. I was transformed from a homophobe, like many in our generation, to a serious supporter of gay and human rights. I can thank Iliff for that. If I had not taken that course and met Charlie I might not have been involved in gay rights."

Steve was a pioneer during a time when people very seldom spoke about gay rights and very few rabbis did it from the pulpit.

(Photo: Gary R. Adler)

But Steve spoke about gay rights during the High Holidays and his leadership allowed gay members of the temple to know they were welcomed. He became a true champion of gay rights.

It also was a pivotal moment for Joyce, who fought for gay rights as an elected official, including same-sex marriage.

Steve was co-chair of the "No on 2" campaign in 1992 when Colorado voters unfortunately approved a constitutional amendment that allowed discrimination against gays and lesbians on such things as employment and housing. The U.S. Supreme Court ruled Amendment 2 unconstitutional in 1996, but Amendment 2 was a horrible black eye for the state when it passed. National boycotts of Colorado hurt our economy and the damage lingered for years.

Our oldest son, David, who was working for the lieutenant governor at the time, also campaigned against Amendment 2. After the election David felt compelled not to give up on

Rabbi Foster often was asked to join elected officials and speak at public rallies that addressed social justice issues. At this 1997 event, sitting behind Steve are (from left to right) Denver Mayor Wellington Webb, Denver City Councilman Dennis Gallagher and Gov. Roy Romer.

educating the public about the dangers of a law that discriminates against a group of people. He organized a trip to Germany called "Journey for Justice," including a visit to the Dachau Concentration Camp Memorial Site, and raised money privately for travel that included journalists from a Denver TV station documenting the journey.

"I called it my Noah's Ark of World Travel because we had two people representing the African-American community, two from the gay and lesbian community, two from the Native American community, two Jews, and it kept going," David said. "I'm sure my dad was the first person I called when I thought about the trip."

Steve joined David on the trip and the delegation also

included a Holocaust survivor and camp liberator. The documentary brought home for Coloradans the destruction caused by the Holocaust and how similar things can happen when one group is targeted for discrimination.

Steve also supported a Jewish group that started a synagogue for gays and lesbians in Denver. Steve gave the group permission to use the chapel at Temple Emanuel for their services.

He also went to bat for an assistant rabbi candidate who told him during a job interview that she was a lesbian. Initially, Steve thought the pretty woman would be a good match for our son, David, who was single at the time, and then she told him she was gay.

The woman went through the job interview with the board and we were all upfront about her being gay. Two very conservative members opposed hiring her.

> Steve: "I said to them that if you as a board don't want to hire her for a legitimate reason, I'll back that. But if you don't want to offer her the job because she is gay then you will also be looking for a new rabbi. It is the only time I did that. They offered her the job but she and her partner decided to stay in New York."

That experience showed Steve that the board needed more education about gays and lesbians because the issue likely was going to surface again. He put together a daylong retreat and invited lay people from a synagogue in New York to talk about their experiences hiring gay people.

Steve: "Obviously, we were not prepared to address the issue and I wanted us to be prepared for the future."

In 1999, following the shootings at Columbine High School, Steve joined hundreds of protestors, including future state Senator Lucia Guzman (to his left), who marched against the National Rifle Association for refusing to cancel its convention in Denver, which took place just a few days after the tragedy.

As the years went on, gay members of our congregation became more comfortable and we hired other gay employees.

Steve: "It took time. These things are not happening overnight. Iliff changed my life and therefore it changed the life of the congregation. No question about that."

Temple Emanuel also was the first synagogue in Colorado to hire a female rabbi. Eve Ben-Ova was hired as our educational director and rabbi.

Steve: "Hiring a female rabbi was a risk because this was new for Colorado. And once again we learned that giving everyone an opportunity benefited the congregation."

Another civil rights related issue that took time was the move by the state of Colorado to pass a law recognizing the Martin Luther King, Jr. holiday. Our friend, Wilma Webb, tried to get the law passed several times as a state legislator only to be blocked by Republicans. Finally, in 1984 she got the bill passed and asked Steve to serve on the committee that planned the first official MLK holiday in Colorado.

The committee met for two years planning the inaugural celebration that took place in 1986.

> Steve: "I was on the MLK commission the first years and the very first public interfaith service was at the temple. We had Dave Brubeck (the American jazz musician and composer) in concert and we raised a lot of scholarship money for kids and I am very proud about that. That was a big deal."

Denver has one of the largest MLK Day celebrations in the country as groups from all walks of life typically march from City Park down Colfax Avenue to Civic Center.

Having marched in Selma in 1965 with Dr. King, Steve felt great pride in being asked to give the invocation for years at Civic Center at the end of the march. For many years, we marched with thousands of people who came together in unity to celebrate Dr. King's legacy.

Yet when Steve believed the inclusiveness of the event was blurred by groups of conservative Christians, he no longer felt he could participate.

> Steve: "I walked off the platform one year and I said to Wellington, I can't do it anymore because there were people

Joyce won her first election to the Denver City Council on June 15, 1993.

shouting, 'Who is for Jesus raise your hand!' It no longer was about inclusion. For my personal integrity I could no longer participate."

Politics also plays a role in the annual celebration especially when the march lands during an election year.

Joyce: "I marched with Steve during the first year and for years after. And you would always know when there was an election year. There were more people marching and more people trying to get to the front row so that they could get their photograph in the newspaper linked arm and arm with the true civil rights activists. The people who were real civil rights leaders showed up every year. Then all of a sudden there were politicians who joined the march because it was a campaign opportunity for them."

The MLK celebration in Denver still is very important; but occasionally, important events like these get hijacked by special interest groups.

In the early years, we marched as the rabbi and the rebbetzin but by 1993 Joyce got an additional title: Denver City Council representative.

Prior to 1993, Joyce never imagined she would be a politician. The first time she went to a Denver City Council meeting before she was elected was after state voters approved Amendment 2. Steve went before the council to encourage the city to enact a new law that at least would protect gays and lesbians who lived in Denver.

Denver is a home-rule city, which means its laws supersede state law. Denver did enact the new law to protect gays and lesbians.

Joyce recalls feeling proud watching Steve testify on behalf of the protection law but she really had no clue how city government operated. Little did she know just a few years later she'd be the one voting on laws as the city's first Jewish councilwoman.

Our son, David, was instrumental in getting Joyce to run for the council in 1993. By then Wellington Webb had served two years as mayor. He appointed Councilwoman Stephanie Foote as his chief of staff, so that left an opening on the council. Stephanie was our council representative and David considered running for the seat but his age excluded him.

He missed the minimum age requirement to serve on the city council by only two months.

That left David and his friend, political consultant Ken Smith,

Joyce was all smiles after her second swearing-in ceremony in 1995 at Civic Center (behind her is Councilwoman Polly Flobeck).

Joyce is proud of many accomplishments on the council, including beginning the first free shuttle from University Hills to Cherry Creek, called the B Line, with the support of Councilwoman Susan Casey (left). War veterans also honored her for helping them relocate their hall in southeast Denver.

scrambling to find another candidate. They both had organized and directed several local campaigns and worked together on former U.S. Senator Bob Kerry's failed presidential bid.

"Joyce really had no experience working with the city council or interfacing with them," Smith recalled. "It was just a little bit out of her comfort zone so there was a large learning curve. But the good news was she had a good base of people to support her; obviously coming from the Jewish community, there was a strong base of Jewish voters. They loved Joyce and they had seen her work in different capacities, whether as the rebbetzin or at Jewish Family Service."

David and Ken teamed up with Colorado State Senator Ken Gordon, a friend of the Foster family, and asked Joyce if she would run for the council seat.

Joyce: "I said, 'Are you kidding me?' I didn't even know how many people sat on the city council. I didn't know anything about city government."

But then David started reminding Joyce that she had several concerns in her district, such as the need to renovate a once popular shopping center, needed improvements to a popular park, and her support of Light Rail.

Joyce: "Steve encouraged me big time, he really did."

Joyce also spoke to her family and friends before making a decision.

"I really encouraged her to do it," said Yana Vishnitsky, her colleague at JFS. "She needed to shine on her own and sometimes with a powerful spouse she didn't have the chance. She needed this to incorporate into her marriage."

The first reaction from Joyce's sister, Sharon, was: "Are you crazy?" But then she and her husband, Joel, came out during the campaign and helped, including waving large campaign signs on street corners on Election Day.

Joyce's boss let her use vacation time to campaign and told her that her job would be waiting if she lost.

Mayor Webb also wanted Joyce to run. Even though we had a friendship with Wellington and Wilma, Steve did not initially support Webb in the 1991 race. Denver District Attorney Norm Early, also African-American, had a sizeable lead in the polls just six months before the election and most of the city's clergy had backed Early.

Webb mounted a comeback and beat Early in a run-off election. He then invited Steve and other religious leaders to give prayers at his historic inauguration.

"It really ended up that Steve was our go-to guy in the Jewish community," Webb said. "We shared the same interest; we fought for the same principles. When the rockets were falling in Israel I went to the synagogue. I didn't go there to make a speech or say anything. My presence was saying, I was here to support you.

"When the council seat opened we supported Joyce because we knew she was a fabulous candidate. We also knew what we would be getting because we expected her to fight like hell for her district, and she did."

With the overwhelming support, Joyce decided to run.

Joyce: "If I knew then what I know now – what it takes to run a campaign – I would have been more afraid. I think ignorance is bliss."

Joyce often says one of her strengths is acknowledging when she doesn't know something and surrounding herself with smart people. And she did that for the campaign. She reached out to Carol Boigon, a political consultant who was well versed on city government.

"At the time, this was all new to Joyce," Boigon recalled. "She didn't know how city government worked or how to debate. But she did have a long list of things she wanted to do – a good housekeeping list. She needed to learn how to present the list."

Joyce's sense of humor helped make her likeable, Boigon said, but debates were initially a challenge.

"She could have the room rolling in stitches but a candidate debate was challenging and different and she was nervous about it," Boigon said.

Joyce was so nervous about the debates that she lost 15 pounds during the 12-week campaign.

> Steve: "I'd be waiting to take her to a debate and she'd be
> in the bathroom with an upset stomach."

But then Joyce hit a subject during a debate at Thomas Jefferson High School that caught the attention of a Rocky Mountain News reporter. Our daughter, Debbie, was a senior there and some neighbors wanted to close the campus so that the students couldn't leave at lunchtime. They complained of trash and kids roaming through the neighborhood.

> Joyce: "There were five of us candidates at the debate and I
> was the only one who questioned why they should close the
> campus. The other four were pandering to the neighbors.

Joyce's position on the city council allowed us to meet President Bill Clinton when he was in Denver on Aug. 13, 1993 for Pope John Paul II's visit for World Youth Day. On another visit, Joyce's mother, Beverly, was thrilled when First Lady Hillary Clinton graciously posed for a photograph (facing page, top). In the 1980s, we also got to meet and visit with Sen. Ted Kennedy during his visit to Denver (facing page, bottom).

I said let's work with the student council and school administration to fix the problems. Kevin Flynn of the Rocky Mountain News covered the debate and the next day he wrote a wonderful piece that said if you're a kid at Thomas Jefferson High School you'd want Joyce Foster to represent you. Of course, high school students don't vote but their parents got the message that on city council I would never pander; I would look for ways to fix things."

She campaigned door-to-door and spent about the same time on the phone raising money for the campaign.

Joyce: "A couple of times people said to me that my background doesn't say I should be in politics. And I said, 'Really?' I was a rabbi's wife for 25 years and I certainly understand politics – synagogue politics; Hello! I listen to people. I care about people. I worked for Jewish Family Service. I care about a lot of issues. I told everyone I was going to win, even though I didn't really believe it, and most of the time my stomach was in knots because I was so nervous."

Carol Boigon also believed Joyce's background would help her as a city council member.

"As a rebbetzin you have to be able to manage families in times of crisis, in times of celebration – and at times make peace," Boigon said.

How thrilled we were when Joyce got the majority of the vote among the five candidates and she didn't face a run-off. We had a block party and Mayor Webb and Wilma joined the celebration.

Steve beamed with pride the night Joyce was elected to the city council, but the dynamic of our marriage changed. Instead of Joyce merely being known as Mrs. Foster, the rabbi's wife, she was now Councilwoman Foster, with people returning her calls and asking her advice.

Joyce: "I mean, if we're really going to be honest in all of this, all of a sudden I had press coverage. You know. I had power. He had his own power and now I had my own power. We did have struggles in terms of why I had to go somewhere at night. Why did I have to take another phone call? Did we work it out? Ultimately we did, because we are still together. There are a lot of couples in politics who are divorced. But it took its toll, it really did."

For Steve, it wasn't so much that she had the limelight, because he always was pointing out to people that Joyce was a city councilwoman. It was more that he felt that when they were in a crowd the conversation always got steered to city politics.

> Steve: "Half of the time it was self-directed (by Joyce) at political stuff in order to get the conversation moving in that direction. And that is true. She can deny it all she wants. She doesn't see it that way but that is true, although not always. Other people asked her, of course. But very, very often it was her talking about city council."

Our son, Danny, saw that dynamic.

"He'll be so supportive of my mom and then he'll be, oh God, another city council story," Danny said. "Sitting around a table he may be rolling his eyes but then in public he is very supportive and cried when she won. He was always 'The MAN' and now he was kind of Mr. Joyce Foster."

Sharon Elfenbein, who came to work for Joyce in 1995, often spoke to family members when they called Joyce at the office.

"When Steve called he expected Joyce to drop everything and speak with him," Sharon said. "That made things uncomfortable for me. I knew Joyce was doing important things in meetings yet he expected me to get her on the phone."

For the next 10 years we shared the limelight and were

viewed by many as the Jewish power couple of Denver. But when Joyce was asked to run for the Colorado Senate in 2008 – the same year she encouraged Steve to announce his retirement in two years – half of the power couple was not "a happy camper."

4

Blending Politics
and Religion

The Keys to Our Successes

Neither one of us grew up in a particularly political family.

Joyce: "We knew we were Democrats growing up. I knew
I was for Adlai Stevenson (in the 1952 presidential race)
but I'm not sure if I really knew who he was."

Steve's family also endorsed Adlai Stevenson even though
just for fun he had an "I Like Ike" poster in his bedroom for
Republican candidate and future President Dwight D.
Eisenhower.

More than politics, the two big issues for both of our families were the Holocaust and the establishment of Israel in 1948.
We grew up hearing about European Jews who fled to the U.S.

from Nazi Germany and those who died in the Holocaust. We remember efforts to raise money for the families who relocated and for needs in Israel, including arms to strengthen the military.

We understood the real threat Israel faced from surrounding Arab countries and the importance of the U.S. financial and political support for Israel. Over the years, we watched Israel grow from 250,000 Jews to more than six million.

That's why our first trip to Israel was such an emotional, important part of our lives. Some of Steve's classmates during graduate school went to live in Israel after the Six Day War in 1967. We were living in a small apartment in Cincinnati and we had no financial means to make the trip. Besides, it would have meant extending Steve's studies another year, and five years was already a huge commitment.

In 1973, we were settled in Denver when the Yom Kippur War really put Israel in danger. The United Jewish Appeal helped raise money in the U.S. to send to Israel. We made a $1,000 donation, which was quite large for us at the time because Steve was only making about $15,000 a year as an assistant rabbi.

A few months later we made our first trip to Israel in 1974 with about 40 members of temple. It was such an amazing trip because as children we never thought we would ever get there. Steve often is overcome with emotion because of the significance of Israel to us personally and as Jews.

> Steve: "Look, I was born in 1943 and by the time I was in Sunday school all that was being spoken about was the Holocaust and the start of Israel in 1948. So, I grew up with all these images of Jews. We lost six million Jews in

the Holocaust and we still move forward. That has always played a profound effect on my life."

Our first trip to Israel in 1974 coincided with the Central Conference of American Rabbis convention and some of us had a chance to hear Prime Minister Golda Meir speak. We have a photograph of her smoking a cigarette next to us. We also felt another connection to Meir because after she emigrated from Russia she lived in the same community of Milwaukee as Steve's grandfather and father and as an adult she lived in Denver for a short time.

Our trip also included being among the first tour buses allowed back in the Golan Heights after the Yom Kippur War. Our bus driver had to sign a piece of paper that we later learned said the Israeli government took no responsibility for our safety. We saw Israeli soldiers who hadn't seen any tourists in six months. From our bus windows we threw out gifts to the Israeli soldiers, including cigarettes and candy. Some of us even gave them our sweaters and coats.

We had a terrific driver on our first trip, Avi Hershkovitz, who later became our regular guide when we took other groups to Israel or for family trips. Overall, the trips were very inspirational but one memory still upsets Steve. His grandfather, Aaron, who came from Eastern Europe, gave Steve his Tefillin, which is a Jewish prayer aid that men wear on their forehead and forearm with a box that contains verses of the Torah. Steve, who as a Reform Jew didn't practice wearing a Tefillin, wore his grandfather's Tefillin at the Western Wall for prayer in honor of his grandfather, who never got to visit Israel.

We've made many trips to Israel as a couple, with members of our congregation, and Steve with his work on different boards. During one trip in the 1990s, we helped plant trees. Steve always sat at the front of the bus during our trips to explain to our fellow travelers where we were headed and why it was important. Our Israeli guide, Avi Hershkovitz, helped us learn about the country and became our friend along with his wife, Judith. In 2007, we invited Christian clergy in

Denver and members of their congregations: a group photograph on Mount Olives, overlooking Jerusalem, included Rev. Bill Calhoun of Montview Boulevard Presbyterian (second right, first row) and Rev. John Bell of Wellshire Presbyterian (third left, first row).

Joyce is our travel agent, helping us to find good deals on trips and being known as an expert suitcase packer.

Steve: "It was really important to me, and some black-hat orthodox Jew came up to me and said I wasn't wearing it right and it wasn't tight enough. He grabbed the straps and started pulling. He grabbed them and it just took that moment away. I still think about it."

Steve has made more than 30 trips to Israel since 1974, including his work with the Jewish Federations of North America, previously called United Jewish Appeal. The national group represents 153 Jewish Federations and raises more than $1 billion annually for social welfare, social services, and educational needs.

Shortly before Steve retired, he was named president of the rabbinic cabinet for Jewish Federations of North America.

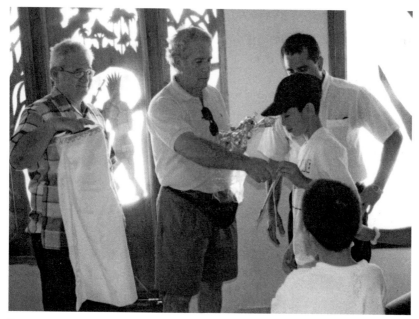

During a visit to a synagogue in Cuba, Steve gave the president of the congregation and members gifts for their synagogue, including a torah cover and havadalah set: Kiddush cup, candle holder, spice box and plate.

Joyce has been to Israel at least 20 times between her work leading groups and trips with family. We have never let safety issues keep us away, but during the 1982 war in Lebanon Steve left a group trip to visit northern Israel and Lebanon near the border with some United Jewish Appeal colleagues.

The UJA colleagues met a few days near the border and Steve went with them before rejoining his group from Denver in Israel.

> Steve: "I was never worried about my safety even with the war in 1982 in Lebanon, but we witnessed a terrorist captured in front of our bus."

All three of our children studied in Israel for a few months when they were in high school and Debbie spent her junior year of college there. At one time, she seriously thought about becoming a rabbi. Israeli Prime Minister Yitzhak Rabin was assassinated in Tel Aviv on November 4, 1995, when Debbie was there for her year of college.

> Joyce: "This was when the buses were getting blown up and we went to visit her and I told her she was coming home. She said, 'I'm not coming home; I am fine.' But I gave her extra money to take cabs and told her she was never to get on another bus."

Later, we learned she pocketed the extra cash and continued to ride the buses with her friends.

"My dad and I exchanged a lot of emails because he was the one person who could understand the passion I had living in Israel and everyone else wanted me to come home," Debbie said. "It was nice to have that understanding because other people couldn't see why I wanted to stay in a place of war but he understood. I really looked forward to getting those emails from him."

We took other trips with members of our congregation.

> Steve: "There is nothing like it – whether we went to Israel or Prague or Cuba – to develop relationships. Your congregants get to know you better and you them. That is a bit of advice for other clergy."

> Joyce: "You are eating together; you're on a bus together; and you are seeing people in a different light."

As part of his work with the Jewish Federations of North America, Steve also made some historic, emotional trips with

Jews immigrating to Israel from the Soviet Union, Ethiopia, and Sarajevo. Steve served on the JFNA cabinet for several years and for two years was chair of the group.

> Steve: "I traveled on a plane to Israel from Ethiopia with a whole plane load of Ethiopian Jews and about 10 lay people."

> Joyce: "That was a very significant and emotional trip for Steve. I didn't go, but he shared the experience with me. The Ethiopians were very poor people and many were wearing a suit for the first time. They were sitting on the plane, in their new suits, and the price tags were still on."

> Steve: "Fifty thousand-plus Jews came from Ethiopia to Israel. The Israeli government wanted to save the Ethiopian Jews, although some black-hat orthodox rabbis didn't consider them Jews. But they were Jews. There was a little window of opportunity to get them out. The Israeli government and Ethiopian government worked out a deal."

The Jews from Sarajevo (during the 1992-1996 war) were fewer in number but they wanted to leave their country because of the war.

Before this trip, Steve called a former classmate who now lived in Vienna, the Austrian capital. She told him to call if he was ever in the country, because they had remained friends.

Steve first met Swanee Hunt when they were both doctoral students at the Iliff School of Theology in Denver. Their professor, Larry Graham, asked them to read their doctoral papers to the class for feedback. Swanee titled her paper: "Religion of the Rich and Super Rich."

We were honored when Swanee Hunt invited us to her swearing-in ceremony for U.S. Ambassador of Austria on Nov. 4, 1993 in Washington, D.C.

Steve didn't know anything about Swanee's background. She dressed casually and blended in with the rest of their classmates.

> Steve: "Swanee certainly didn't appear to be rich, so my question was, how could she know and write about the rich and super rich. Then she told me her father was H.L. Hunt (a Texas oilman and billionaire) and I said, 'The H.L. Hunt who is an anti-Semite?' "

Swanee wasn't upset by my comment and we became friends. Her father was a conservative Republican but Swanee is a Democrat and humanitarian.

By 1993, Swanee had been appointed by President Clinton as the U.S. ambassador to Austria. At her invitation, we attended her swearing-in ceremony in Washington, D.C. Once she heard Steve was coming to Vienna, she made memorable plans for him and the other travelers.

> Steve: "The bus arrived from Sarajevo in Vienna and Swanee had lunch ready for us at the embassy. And she also invited Simon Wiesenthal, the famous Nazi hunter who was living in Vienna at the time. It was a great scene of rabbis eating lunch together and visiting with Wiesenthal."

> Joyce: "Steve was at the center of several civil rights and human rights movements here and in Europe over a span of 30 years. He marched in Selma in 1965 and then played a role during significant immigrations to Israel in the 1970s, '80s and '90s."

Experiencing firsthand the emotional resettling of Jews in Israel added to Steve's unshakable support of Israel. And he felt it was important to bring Christian clergy and members of their congregations to Israel to help them better understand the importance of Israel. We invited members of both the Montview Boulevard and Wellshire Presbyterian churches in Denver to make the trip.

"We talked and talked and talked about many issues over coffee, including Israel, as we got to know each other," said Rev. Bill Calhoun, who was a pastor at Montview Presbyterian. "Our trip to Israel helped Jews and Presbyterians better understand each other."

> Steve: "I wanted Jews to understand what Christians meant when they spoke about 'The Holy Land' and I

wanted Christians to understand what we Jews mean when we speak about 'the state of Israel.' It was life-changing, it really was. For me, I was always preaching to the choir – my own Jewish choir – and now I had an opportunity to talk and show ministers and lay people."

Rev. Peter Eaton, the former Dean of Saint John's Episcopal Cathedral in Denver, didn't go on our trips to Israel but he and Steve often discussed the topic.

"I learned a lot from Steve over the years about Israel and contemporary Jewish life," Eaton said. "We could disagree but it was important to have the conversation with Steve and learn from him. He is a leading light in Jewish education in America and an important voice."

In Denver, Steve continually pushed for more interfaith dialogue and worked with Baptists, Catholics, Methodists, Presbyterians, and other faith leaders on a variety of social justice issues. Calhoun often took topics of their discussions and wrote about social justice issues in Montview's weekly bulletin.

The religious leaders also formed friendships.

"I always call Steve my pastor because in relationship to other clergy he reached out to me more during my health issues," Calhoun said. "He seemed to care the most and he listens the most."

Those friendships even survived disagreements, such as in 1986 when Steve testified in district and federal court against the city sponsoring a nativity scene outside the Denver City and County Building. Steve testified that it was a conflict between church and state for the Christian symbol to be placed outside the public building every Christmas season. His clergy friends,

Our trip to Kolin, Czechoslovakia was very important. Nazis robbed items from this synagogue and others in Europe during World War II. Steve tracked down the Kolin items in Switzerland and the rescued artifacts are now in the Temple Emanuel chapel in Denver.

Catholic Auxiliary Bishop George Evans of the Archdiocese of Denver and Father George Neofotistos of the Greek Orthodox Church, testified that the nativity scene was not a religious symbol but a secular symbol of a national holiday.

The local Jews loved that Steve had the courage to testify even in the face of death threats. The Anti-Defamation League, however – which provided public relations for the Allied Jewish Federation at the time – was not pleased. The ADL wanted Jews to stay out of the issue, but for Steve it was a blatant disregard for the separation of church and state.

The courts disagreed and the nativity scene, now battered by age, still goes up each year at the City and County Building.

It was a thrill to meet author and Nobel Peace Prize recipient Elie Wiesel when he visited the University of Denver Center for Judaic Studies in 1987. Wiesel, a survivor of the Nazi concentration camps, was awarded the Nobel Peace Prize for his message of peace, atonement and human dignity to humanity.

While Bishop Evans and Steve disagreed on that issue, their friendship lasted until his death. Evans was the right-hand man for Archbishop James Casey.

Steve: "George was very sick and I went to see him in the hospital and told him I was going to Israel. I asked him if he wanted me to bring him back a cross and have it blessed by the Roman Catholics or the Orthodox Greeks. He said both. So, when we were in Bethlehem I got him a nice big cross and had it blessed by the Catholics and Greeks at the Church of the

Nativity. I brought it back to George. He thanked me and about two weeks later he died."

Steve was asked to give the eulogy at Bishop Evans' funeral. As is tradition in the Catholic faith, there was an open casket and Bishop Evans was holding the cross that Steve gave him.

Friendships are important among clergy of different faiths because not only can we relate to each other as individuals and what we face as clergy, but as a group we also can promote social change.

Steve worked with Bishop Evans, Rev. Jim Peters of New Hope Baptist, and Rev. Gil Horn, co-pastor of Montview Presbyterian, to start the Denver Area Interfaith Clergy Conference.

> Steve: "It was a dream of mine that we would not just have an East Denver Ministerial Alliance but a citywide group of like-minded and progressive-minded clergy who would talk to each other and be responsive to issues."

The Denver Area Interfaith Clergy Conference eventually disbanded as members died and there was no full-time director. But that didn't stop Steve from standing with other clergy on many social issues, including gang violence, opposition to the death penalty, and support of new gun laws.

As clergy, we knew not all of our congregants were going to agree with our stances on such issues.

"Obviously, any time you take a political stand you lose some members and you gain some members," said Janet Bronitsky, executive director of Temple Emanuel, who worked with Steve for 20 years. "I would say it was all a wash. People just expected Rabbi Foster to be in the forefront of whatever was going on and that was just the nature of him. So there were people who loved him and people who loved to hate him and that's just the way it was. For whatever reasons they loved his sermons or hated his sermons, they just knew he was going to be politically involved."

In 1998, a group of liberal clergy started the Interfaith Alliance of Colorado. The idea arose after Steve spoke at a memorial dinner for Rev. Horn, who died at age 57 from cancer.

> Steve: "I spoke about how we had given up to the right-wing and it was dictating what was going on in the community. We started a Colorado chapter of the Interfaith Alliance and it allows liberal religious people – not just clergy – to have a unified voice."

The Denver clergy also worked together on projects that benefited the community, including Habitat for Humanity. Steve was asked to organize synagogues and churches in Denver's Hilltop neighborhood and volunteers from the congregations came together.

> Steve: "We had an interfaith group that built a home in 2000 and it was for a Muslim family. That was good."

The clergy also rallied in times of crisis. During a massive blizzard in 1982, more than 25 inches of snow brought Denver and surrounding cities to a standstill. Catholic priest Charles Woodrich, "Father Woody," reached out to the community to raise emergency funds to help the homeless. Steve stepped up and brought him a $5,000 check – the first large donation the priest received.

But some disagreements with clergy we considered friends left scars. Knowing our deep commitment to Israel, it hurt when Presbyterian Church (U.S.A.) voted in 2014 to divest from three U.S. companies the group said does business in Israel.

Besides working with other clergy, Steve was called upon to help during violent murders that strongly impacted the community. During the tragic Columbine High School shootings in 1999 two classmates killed 12 students and a teacher on April 20 before killing themselves. Another 21 students were injured, some paralyzed by the bullets.

The mother of one of the shooters was Jewish and her attorney asked Steve to meet with her and her husband.

At the time, this was the worst high school mass killing and the world's media was in town. There also was a barrage of questions about how the parents of the shooters did not know what their sons had planned.

> Steve: "The mother came into my office two or three times. She was struggling because of what her son had done and the fact that he also died. I was speaking to her as a rabbi, to a mother who had just lost her son. To me, that is what it was all about. It wasn't her fault, even though some people were questioning what caused her son to do what he did. I didn't think about who was at fault but rather wanted to help this woman who was suffering."

In 1984, despite some opposition at the temple, Steve performed a funeral for liberal radio talk show host Alan Berg when he was assassinated by white supremacists in his driveway. Steve gave one of the eulogies.

Steve: "We had extra security because our synagogue, being the largest, is a target. There have been times we had swastikas painted on it but we didn't seek publicity when it happened, because we didn't want copycats."

Joyce also developed strong relationships with other clergy, which helped during her campaigns. She encouraged all segments of the community – including leadership of the Denver Public Schools – to include clergy in discussions. One example was when DPS Superintendent Michael Bennet, who went on to become a U.S. senator, decided to temporarily close a predominantly minority high school without extensive public input. The school needed to be reorganized to address such issues as low test scores and high drop-out rates.

The school had several prominent alumni, including Wellington and Wilma Webb, who ended up protesting the closing with black clergy at the superintendent's office.

Joyce: "I realized early on while on the council that initiating any major event to have the community representatives at the table early. Michael Bennet knew that but realized he just had to add additional leaves to that table, especially when dealing with school issues."

Bennet listened and included the community at large in the closing process. And his decision proved to be the right one with the high school reopening a few years later.

Other emotional issues split the community, including the clergy. Steve and some clergy disagreed on a number of topics, from women's reproduction rights to gay rights to decriminalizing marijuana.

Steve: "I was the first clergy person to come out in favor of decriminalizing marijuana. Why should all of these black and Hispanic kids who can't afford good attorneys be in jail for smoking grass? I'm not a smoker; that's not been part of my life. But we had too many minority kids in jail for smoking pot."

Joyce: "More cities and states are going to decriminalize it, too."

Steve: "One day every state will allow gays and lesbians to marry, as they should. That's a much bigger issue than marijuana."

We agree you cannot pick and choose when it comes to civil rights issues.

Steve: "Prejudice is prejudice. Jews have faced prejudice and that is why it makes us so sensitive to the prejudices against other people. Who helped start the NAACP (National Association for the Advancement of Colored People)? I'm talking about in the civil rights movement era. It was Jews who helped finance it, and Jews who helped to bring people along who encouraged civil rights. Who is behind the civil rights movement when it comes to gays and lesbians? To a great measure it is Jews, because we have been there."

Another bone of contention for Steve is the Colorado Legislature's practice – like many elected groups nationally including the U.S. Congress – starting each day with a prayer.

The lawmakers invite clergy from throughout the area to have a short prayer. Some lawmakers disagree with the practice as a violation of the separation of church and state and stay out of the chambers until the prayer is over.

But Joyce felt that would be rude and was in her seat each day to hear the prayer after she was elected to the Colorado state senate in 2008. That didn't keep her from educating the Christian ministers that while she supported their prayers, she would be more supportive if they did not finish the prayers with the Christian "in the name of our Lord and Savior Jesus Christ. Amen."

> Steve: "We can't say Amen to that. The word Amen means to affirm. I cannot affirm that which I can't affirm. People don't realize that – and some people don't understand that."

At one time, a rabbi was the chaplain of the state senate and part of the prayer rotation. Joyce invited several rabbis to say the prayer, including a reluctant Steve.

> Steve: "We have a slight disagreement about this and I'm the hypocrite. I very seldom did the prayer. I didn't want to do it. I told them I don't want to do it. I said, don't call me. But when she was in the senate they called me every first session. 'Would you please do it? Joyce is here,' blah, blah, blah. ..."

> Joyce: "I was proud. I wanted him to be there. He gave the best one."

That pride extends to how we work individually as leaders. For Steve, his leadership skills were evident early in his career when he took on projects at the temple and preached, with no fear, about social justice issues.

For Joyce, the leadership skills would really surface once she was elected to the City Council. As a rabbi's wife she purposely did not take a leadership role at the temple.

Joyce: "I never took a leadership role at temple because I felt that was a conflict of interest with Steve being the rabbi. And I think a lot of spouses make a big mistake in taking a leadership role, like becoming the president of the Sisterhood or another group. I just think it is a conflict with their spouse."

Steve: "And a conflict with the lay people."

Joyce: "Yes, let the lay people be chairs. I'd help them find a speaker or do other things when they asked, but let them be the leaders."

Joyce was often asked to speak at Sisterhood events over the years. In a Sisterhood installation in 2012, Joyce emphasized the need for women to carve out time for themselves, something she learned over the years.

"On the plane the flight attendant talks about in case of an emergency you need to put the oxygen mask on yourself before you help someone else," Joyce told members of the Sisterhood. "We need to extend that rule to ourselves. We all need to find balance in our lives to be successful. For us to be successful in our family life, career, volunteer experience, we need to first put on our oxygen mask. ... We need to be honest about our time, sometimes we need to say no, especially if we feel a little off balance. We will be much more productive and effective if we take the opportunity to evaluate our needs."

Joyce took heed of that lesson in 1993 when she suddenly was in a leadership role as one of 13 city council members who passed laws and were featured almost daily in the city's two newspapers, The Denver Post and Rocky Mountain News.

In 1993, the newspapers were in a so-called war, trying to out-scoop each other to build circulation and try to run one another out of business. That meant both papers had teams of reporters at city hall looking for headlines.

The journalists didn't have to look far. In 1993, the city faced gang violence where children were being shot; the construction of a new airport that faced controversy and opening delays; and the arrival of Pope John Paul II for World Youth Day.

Joyce was in office only a few weeks when a group of her constituents called her office and complained they were being overrun with prairie dogs. The residents lived along the route where the Catholic pilgrims would walk to the Pope's outdoor Mass at a state park.

Some neighborhoods were surrounded by open fields with the small, burrowing animals. The neighbors said the prairie dogs, which are considered large rodents, were digging into their backyards. They worried that their children would be exposed to fleas and possibly rabies from the prairie dogs.

Joyce gathered her staff, made a few calls to city officials, and found out the city had no policy concerning the removal of prairie dogs. Some communities were trapping and relocating the animals but that was expensive.

Joyce made the decision to have the parks department euthanize and remove the animals.

> Joyce: "We knew they were rodents and we knew they could carry bubonic plague. To me it came down to the safety of children."

Once the process got underway Joyce received an urgent page that there was trouble at the site. The police and fire departments were there along with protestors from PETA (People for the Ethical Treatment of Animals).

> Joyce: "I drove out there and a woman yelled, 'Whose decision was it to gas these prairie dogs?' I said it was mine. She then said the prairie dogs have as much right to live as the children and right then I knew the conversation was over. I was never going to convince the PETA people that the prairie dogs were rodents and the children were human beings."

The PETA protestors put up small white crosses that said, "Joyce Foster Nazi." Despite the controversy, Joyce never backed down.

> Joyce: "I was shaking. I was absolutely shaking but these people with their children who lived in the neighborhood were so happy that I stood by the decision. I did not cave in to the people who were shipped in from Boulder to protest. I told them I didn't care if they called me a Nazi, but it was uncomfortable and nasty."

Several years later a firefighter who was at the scene that day recalled it at his retirement party.

> Joyce: "He said it was one highlight of his career when a council person stood up for what was right and took responsibility in front of the protestors. His comments made me feel good because he recognized my decision was based on common sense."

Joyce knew she had a lot to learn about city government and wasn't afraid to ask a lot of questions of city staff.

Steve: "She had a learning curve that was very steep but it wasn't very long before she made a difference on council. She wasn't going to be told what she should say or do and that is her strength. She was not going to cave in to what other people wanted when she knew they were wrong."

Once the prairie dog crisis was addressed, the next question about the Pope's visit came – from Steve.

Steve: "Because I was 'the voice of the Jewish community' I called the priest who was putting the Pope's trip together, and who was also a personal friend, and asked him what's going to happen with the clergy when the Pope came. And he told me, 'Absolutely nothing. The Pope doesn't want to meet with the clergy; he only wants to meet with the kids for World Youth Day.' But the priest said, you'll be different because you're going to be sitting next to Joyce and as a city council member she'll be there. She was the one invited but I got to go, too."

Joyce: "Steve had to brush off his ego a little bit."

Steve: "I don't think so."

Joyce: "Yes, you had to brush off your ego."

We both had to brush off the rain because while we were under a tent when the Pope arrived at the airport we got soaked. We also had to ask organizers if we could be the first to meet President Bill Clinton, who came in Friday night for a dinner. We couldn't attend the dinner because we had services at temple. The organizers got us to the front of the line.

Joyce: "I promised the congregation that if I was elected my role at temple would not change. I never went back on my word. When Denver International Airport finally opened, they had a big party on a Friday night and we couldn't go. Did I want to go? You bet. But what message would I be sending to the Jewish community?"

Whether you are clergy or an elected official your word is what makes or breaks you in the eyes of the public. We know we angered some people but in the end you have to do what you think is right and damn the consequences.

Steve: "The public watches what you say because whether you are a politician or clergy you are judged if you walk the walk or you don't. There is such a thing as personal integrity."

5

Being a Good Leader

Listen, respond,
and be true to yourself

Besides standing up for what you believe in, clergy and politicians have several other things in common when it comes to being good leaders.

We had similar ways of creating the best environment for us to succeed as leaders.

We surrounded ourselves with smart people and let them do their jobs without micromanaging them. We responded to our congregation and constituents in a timely manner. And we had to raise money, which was not always easy and was sometimes somewhat humiliating.

Steve readily admits that Joyce has a special gift when it comes to knowing who to hire.

The one time Steve went against Joyce's instincts and hired an assistant rabbi she thought might not be a good fit, it turned out to be an awful match for Steve and the congregation.

Steve: "My first assistant, Rabbi Rick Shapiro, was really good. He was with us for three years and was a little older than the others who applied for the job. Eventually he wanted to go on his own, which I supported. Then we wanted to hire this other guy and Joyce said don't hire him. Joyce was sick and he came over to the house and gave her a hug. She said, 'He's a phony, don't hire him.' So, we hired him. And it was awful. One weekend he disappeared. It was six weeks after he had started and I couldn't find him. He told me he didn't have to tell me where he went. But I needed him. I had four funerals on a Sunday. So, from the very beginning he was a problem."

When his contract was up in three years Steve did not renew it.

> Steve: "At temple, people stay for years. They don't leave. So when someone has to be terminated it really is for cause. People come and they are creative and they do what they want to do. They cooperate and work together and that is what you want: ownership."

Janet Bronitsky, executive director of the temple, worked with Steve from 1990 to 2010.

"Steve is a very creative thinker and great to be around," she said. "He's opinionated, he cares about things and he lets you know what he is thinking."

One of Steve's major fundraising efforts was for an addition at the synagogue. Joining him for a groundbreaking ceremony was (from left to right) Rabbi Eve Ben-Ora, Rabbi Earl Stone, Rabbi Foster and Associate Rabbi Bruce Greenbaum.

Every week, Steve had a staff meeting with the senior staff to listen to their concerns and review his agenda for the week. He did that the entire time he was senior rabbi – even though when Steve was the assistant rabbi there were no weekly staff meetings.

Steve encouraged his staff to go beyond their daily duties and to feel comfortable to be creative and suggest ideas.

Steve: "I don't remember a time when a staff member came to me and asked to do something and I said we couldn't do it. I was never that way. I would say let's try it, let's see. ... There are certain things that the person who is in charge – whether it's the senior rabbi or politician – is responsible for and he or she has a right to set certain conditions on their staff's creativity. But not to allow people to exercise their God-given ability is wrong."

Joyce also surrounded herself with creative people and let them voice their opinions. During her 10 years on city council her staff included Carol Boigon, Sharon Elfenbein, Ken Smith and Shelly Waters.

As a state senator, she relied on her friend Bonnie Saliman to help her run the office part-time.

Joyce valued her staff's opinions.

"Controversial subjects would come up on the council and she was exceptionally good about putting the right people together and sitting them around the table," said Ken Smith, who helped run her first campaign and went to work for her full-time in 1995. "She used her best sort of Jewish mom skills to extract the best from everyone around the table. So, everyone left the table feeling they were heard and their opinions and expertise valued. Maybe they didn't get everything or even half of what they wanted but they believed she listened and that was one of her secrets to success."

As a new councilwoman, Joyce readily accepted that she had a lot to learn about city government and welcomed city staff to her office for "brown bag" lunches. They brought their lunches to her office and got to know her over the meals. In the meantime, she got a crash course on city government.

Joyce: "At first, I didn't even know what questions to ask on things like city bonds so I brought the experts to my office to learn. If I didn't like their answers I sought other

people out. I knew I had to be prepared before I was at a public hearing."

While Joyce listened to her staff and public employees, they knew she was no pushover.

"Joyce was very determined in a way that may surprise people who didn't know her," Smith said. "She certainly respected everyone's opinion but don't fool yourself if she didn't agree. If she felt the city staff was off-base or just comfortable with the same old way of doing something she would be the first to challenge and push back. But she would do it with respect and they would love her for it."

Sharon Elfenbein said she wasn't just Joyce's employee but part of a team. When Sharon saw a problem in the community, such as the need to complete the Cherry Creek bike trail, she would bring the issue to Joyce.

"She let us come up with our own ideas and she supported them. We were always a team. She was the leader but she listened to us," Sharon said.

Joyce easily won re-election in 1995. Voters in her district saw how during her first two years in office Joyce fought hard for issues in southeast Denver.

"Joyce governed with the thoughts of how people lived, how they worked, and what would make the city better," Boigon said. "It was an active approach to government about such things as getting the garbage picked up and the other things that affect daily life; because if you don't pay attention neighborhoods can get neglected and go into triage. Joyce did not allow that to happen."

Joyce is joined by area residents looking at a plaque that honors her work on the Denver City Council and the University Hills Shopping Center renovation.

We both had to raise money in our jobs, whether it was to help the congregation grow or support the Stepping Stones program or to run a political campaign. Some people are good at raising money and some are not. But if clergy or politicians want to survive and grow, fundraising is part of the job.

> Steve: "I was never afraid to raise money, because I was not asking for myself. Being a rabbi or clergy is like being a president of a college. A president who doesn't raise money should be fired because that is part of his or her job."

Over 40 years, Steve raised about $12 million for such projects as new offices, a redecorated social hall, Shwayder Camp, and a new chapel and new classroom wing at Temple Emanuel.

The temple's Feiner Family Chapel is dedicated to the preservation of our rich Jewish heritage, our legacy and the historical struggle to preserve Judaism. When we were furnishing the chapel, Steve wanted to include Eastern European Jewish artifacts that were stolen and warehoused by the Nazis during World War II.

Steve located furniture and symbols that were taken from a small synagogue in Kolin, Czechoslovakia. The artifacts hold the memories of the 430 Jews who lived in Kolin and were taken to Nazi concentration camps. Only 16 of those Jews survived and returned to Kolin.

The religious symbols from Kolin are united in the chapel with furnishings from the sanctuary from the former Temple Emanuel on Pearl Street in Denver. In 1989, Steve traveled to Switzerland to purchase the historic furniture that was part of the Kolin synagogue.

The Nazis also confiscated Torahs from synagogues throughout Eastern Europe that were recovered and eventually placed in the Westminster Synagogue in London. Steve contacted them and found that three Torahs from Kolin were there. He asked for the most damaged one as a symbol of survival. It now rests in Temple Emanuel's Holy Ark.

We could not have retrieved those items for our chapel without financial support from our congregation.

But raising money is never easy and clergy must be open to every opportunity that benefits their congregations.

Steve jumped at an opportunity when Denver's private Jewish hospital, Rose Hospital founded by a group of Jewish

Steve's work with interfaith marriages and "Stepping Stones to a Jewish Me" hit home when our daughter-in-law, Becky, converted before she married our son, Danny. She signed the ketubah, a traditional Jewish marriage contract, before the wedding ceremony.

businessmen in 1948, was sold to a health conglomerate in 1995 for about $170 million.

From proceeds of the hospital sale, the Rose Foundation was formed and it challenged Jewish groups to develop endowment funds for their own organizations. The foundation would give each group 50 cents for every dollar it raised for endowment purposes. Steve presented the Temple Emanuel board with an idea for lifetime memberships. The lifetime memberships would cost $16,000 and whoever bought them would never have to pay dues. The temple would gain $16,000 upfront plus another $8,000 from the Rose Foundation for each membership, which would more than offset the benefits of the yearly dues.

It was a one-shot deal from the foundation with a deadline to apply.

> Steve: "At first, the board didn't think it would work but I asked them to just let me try. In six months I raised $2 million. I did it myself. It was my idea and I had to sell it to the board. Half of the board members ended up signing for the lifetime memberships. It was an opportunity and I took advantage of it."

He also raised money to expand the temple's Shwayder Camp in the mountains. The camp was large enough for 80 children but we wanted to expand it to serve 120. That led us to raise money for a larger dining hall, expanded staff, and a full-time director.

Joyce's road to raising money for her political campaigns was made a little harder after she was advised by her campaign managers not to take any political action committee (PAC) donations. PACs are organizations that pool campaign contributions from donors – such as the tobacco industry or oil and gas industry. Senator Ken Gordon led the way in refusing PAC donations so he would not be obligated to any special interest group.

Not taking PAC money meant Joyce was on the phone constantly, seeking contributions from individuals. It was familiar territory because she had raised money for Jewish Family Service and other nonprofit organizations, but now she was asking for donations to help her get elected.

Besides raising money, another trait needed for clergy and politicians to be successful is to understand the needs of your staff and your community. And that means you have to be actively participating and not just rely on your staff.

For example, one of Steve's assistants decided he wanted to leave our temple and start his own synagogue. Steve supported him and helped with such things as printing materials until they got established.

Steve later had a discussion with the same rabbi about membership in the new congregation.

> Steve: "I asked if he was trying to get people to belong to his congregation and he said, 'That's not my job. That's the lay people's job.' I said that's not true. It's a community and as much his job as the others'. I think part of the reason he didn't succeed was because he was not willing to get out there and get people to join his synagogue."

Steve was always active in growing the temple and gauging the needs of the congregation.

> Steve: "I always refer to the synagogue like a gas station, a human gas station. Some people come to temple for an overhaul. Sometimes they come in for just a checkup, like to replace their wiper blades or oil. Or they come in for a flat tire. You have to be there like a service station and serve their needs."

The same is true for politicians. Most people couldn't care less about their city council until there's a problem in their neighborhood. But whether it is something small like a park restroom that needs repair or a large issue like a shopping center needing renovation, you need to respond.

Joyce: "Sometimes things fall through the cracks. I'm not perfect, but the goal is to respond to everyone – whether you agree with them or disagree with them."

Denver has a history of strong neighborhood associations and there were 40 different groups in Joyce's district. There also was a history of conflicts among the neighborhoods, prompting Joyce and her staff to work with representatives of each association to head off problems.

"This built relationships and smoked out disputes," Carol Boigon said.

Her office also sent out a newsletter to inform residents about projects underway or completed.

"By the time she left office Joyce had a long list of neighborhood accomplishments," Boigon said. "She was more aggressive on neighborhood issues than any elected official I had ever seen."

And she took on some tough issues, such as getting regulations for tow trucks that were battling for business at accident scenes, and addressing slow response times from city ambulances.

"Joyce would not give up," Boigon said. "She was like a dog shaking a dead animal. She knew people needed to be held accountable and she was willing to go toe-to-toe."

Joyce also fought to get taxicab companies to do a better job of picking up disabled riders. After she raised the issue, the taxi companies added more vans to their fleets.

"She wanted someone who was disabled to be able to pick up the phone like anyone else and get a cab," Sharon Elfenbein said.

One of Joyce's largest battles was getting the city to build a skateboard park for young people. The issue came up at a council hearing about new regulations to keep skateboards off the downtown 16th Street Mall. The pedestrian mall has a lot of concrete, stairs and railings that attracted the skateboarders. City officials complained about the damage to the concrete and business owners were irritated by the presence of the skateboarders.

"I recall telling the council committee that before they further penalize these skateboarders they need to give them a place to go," said Dave Stalls, who ran a nonprofit center for at-risk youth called The Spot. "Joyce listened and thought it just made sense."

But it became a battle, not only with some business owners, but also with her colleagues on the council. The location of a skate park had to be near downtown, which was not Joyce's district. Other council members said the skate park would attract crime but Joyce forged ahead.

Her staff invited youth from the Denver Public Schools to sit on a committee and they reached out to communities in California that already had skateboard parks. But the real test came when Joyce was able to convince Mayor Wellington Webb to put the skate park among several projects in a $100 million bond package.

"It was one of Wellington's great strengths to understand that you had to spread the love to every neighborhood to get a $100 million bond approved by voters," recalled Ken Smith. "The months leading up to what projects would be placed on the bond was a dog fight for Joyce but she never backed down."

Our kids were surprised Joyce went to bat for the skateboard park because when they were younger she was very protective. She didn't want Danny to play football when he was young because of safety issues so he joined the lacrosse team,

(courtesy Kenny Be)

One of Joyce's toughest fights on the Denver City Council was getting the city's first skateboard park built. Artist Kenny Be memorialized her in the weekly newspaper Westword in 2002 (facing page). Mayor Wellington Webb joined her for the ribbon cutting in 2001 along with David Stalls (left) who worked with youth, and teenagers Amberleigh Hammond and Jake Ortiz who helped the city design the facility for nearly four years.

which turned out was even more physical than football.

And skateboarding definitely looked more dangerous to Joyce than any team sport.

"Well, it's funny that she became the driving force for the skateboard park because she wouldn't let us have skateboards as kids," David said. "My mom thought they were way too dangerous. It took me awhile to appreciate her fight for the skate park but it's pretty cool."

There were numerous times Joyce could have gotten discouraged and given up but she forged ahead.

She used her negotiating skills to get the skateboard park on the bond issue and never compromised about the need for the facility or the location.

> Joyce: "Politics is a lot of negotiating and compromising but you can only compromise to a point; you have to stick with what you think is right."

> Steve: "I have to say that the synagogue is the same way. Dealing with a board, you have to compromise but if you compromise too much you are giving away the principle and you don't want to do that. You have to always keep in mind what the principle is. Leadership is about helping people to find a way; that is what it is all about. You can't call yourself a leader if people are not being moved to do something."

> Joyce: "And that really is the difference between a leader and a manager."

Mayor Webb's support for the skateboard park wasn't a surprise, because he had supported Joyce from the start. Shortly into her first term, Mayor Webb found money to pay for her to attend the John F. Kennedy School of Government at Harvard University. She completed the program for senior executives in state and local government in 1994.

"I wanted Joyce to get off to a good start because the more Wilma and I worked with Joyce and Steve over the years, the more we felt they were our friends and part of our political family," Webb said. "Joyce supported me while she was on the council and I supported her."

Joyce faced term limits in 2003 and reluctantly had to leave her council seat. It was hard for her to leave the position because

The majority of the Denver City Council meetings focused on serious issues but council members also celebrated special milestones. In 1998, the Denver Broncos (including team owner Pat Bowlen, far right) and star running back Terrell Davis (second from the right, back row) brought the team's first Vince Lombardi Trophy for its Super Bowl victory to the council chambers to celebrate.

people in the congregation and among Steve's friends and colleagues saw Joyce in a new light and with a different kind of respect.

> Joyce: "I loved being on the city council. When we were at Jewish receptions, bar mitzvahs or weddings, all of a sudden I could actually stand with the guys and they were interested in what I was talking about. Before, I kind of felt invisible at the events but after I was elected to the council people actually came over to me for the first time in all those years and wanted to talk. I loved it. I listened to them and I had something to say. I knew what I was

talking about whether it came to zoning or this or that with the city. Yeah, it was pretty fun."

For those 10 years, business people who had ducked her calls when she was trying to find jobs for her JFS clients now had her number on speed dial.

Joyce: "The same people left meetings to take my calls now and there was a real sense of power. But I used that power, I believe, in very positive ways. I connected Jewish Family Service with the city on programs they should have been applying for but weren't. I reached out to other agencies, too, because I had worked with these organizations and knew they could benefit from city programs and the city could benefit from working with them."

Joyce faced 2003 with a sense of loss about what she would do next. David and Ali had their first child, Abby, and Joyce looked forward to being on grandmother duty when asked. Steve also enjoyed being a grandfather and still was very active at the temple.

The next five years we did our duties as a couple at the temple and in early 2008 Joyce convinced Steve he should then announce his plan to retire in 2010. Steve wasn't anxious to leave but thought it probably was time. The two years would give the temple's board time to do a thorough search for his replacement and get the congregation ready for the transition.

Then something neither of us saw coming upset the apple cart. State Senator Ken Gordon faced term limits and could not run for re-election. Gordon served in the state legislature for 16 years, first as a representative from 1992 to 2000 and then as a

senator from 2001 to 2008. He wanted to make sure his replacement was someone he respected and admired.

Once again Ken Smith and our son, David, joined forces and recruited Joyce to run for the senate seat, much to the chagrin of Steve. This happened after Steve had already sent a letter to the congregation advising them he was retiring in 2010. If he had known Joyce was re-entering politics the letter never would have been sent in 2008.

> Steve: "I'm saying to myself, 'She's the one who just convinced me that I should retire and now she's going back to politics for eight years?' because that's how I saw it. I was frustrated. Why should I retire? I wasn't anxious to retire. I was not a happy camper."

Our sons, David and Danny, with former President Bill Clinton, are active in local and national politics.

Joyce: "He was not happy for four years but I never planned to run for a second term, never. And for the first two years, he was still working and it's really not two full years because the session is only 120 days. I still met with constituents and worked on bills when we were out of public session, but I was available for Steve and the family."

The whole family rallied around her senate campaign and she won by a large margin. But the family noticed the tension between us.

"My dad was winding up his career and probably was thinking, 'What's next? Is she going to run for mayor?' " Danny said. "She could have run for a second term but she always said she was just going to run for one term."

While Joyce enjoyed her senate work, it was different from being on the city council.

As a state senator, Joyce didn't have the budget to hire full-time staff or mail newsletters so she had to rely on her website to update constituents on her work. She liked to inject a little humor in her postings to have her constituents relate to her and keep reading as she updated them on her work.

One example was a Thanksgiving message posted on her site in 2009:

"On Monday I spent the day shopping for a Jell-O mold since I must have given them all away over the years. I found a yummy recipe that I remember making many years ago. I had two of my grandchildren schlepping through every housewares store I knew. Finally my 8-year-old grandson Aiden asked me a great question: Jell-O is good but mold is bad so why would I want to combine the two?"

Many people in her district remember Jell-O molds and hopefully, kept reading her post instead of just hitting the delete button.

Humor can be good for politics and it also helps relieve stress in times of personal crisis.

Just as our lives started to settle into a new routine with Joyce busy with her senate work and Steve busy at the synagogue, we both got blindsided. Steve was preparing for retirement and the congregation was having several salutes and parties. But during his yearly routine physical a doctor discovered Steve had leukemia.

In May 2009, Steve's primary doctor sent him to Dr. Al Feiner, a specialist in hematology and oncology, to have his bone marrow tested. The timing couldn't have been worse because we had several trips planned that summer. In fact, the next day we were traveling to Cincinnati for the ordination of Rabbi Allysa Stanton, the first female African-American rabbi in the U.S., who had worked with Steve in Denver.

After Cincinnati, we had a trip planned to Washington, D.C., where Steve was being installed as chair of the rabbinic cabinet for the Jewish Federations of North America, which was a huge honor.

In July, we were taking a group of 40 people to Israel, including Joyce's sister and brother-in-law.

> Steve: "I had the bone marrow test on a Wednesday or Thursday and we went to Cincinnati the next day. Dr. Feiner said he'd call when he got the bone marrow test results and Joyce and I were in a rental car with a friend in the back seat when he called on my cell phone and told me to get back to Denver. It was bad. So I drove to downtown Cincinnati thinking I am dying and by the time we got out of the car my cell rang again. He sent the results to some-one at Northwestern University for a second opinion and instead of dying I have what they call hairy cell leukemia and on a scale of one to 10 it is the most treatable."

In a span of 20 minutes between the two calls emotions were all over the board.

When we got back to Denver, Dr. Feiner wanted to start chemotherapy right away but Steve wanted to wait until after our Israel trip in July.

Joyce: "Steve tells Dr. Feiner he really can't do anything until the end of July and Dr. Feiner is hilarious. He said, 'Oh, okay, the rabbi here is too busy to have cancer so we can't do anything until the end of July because he is too busy to have cancer. Cancer, go away until the end of July.' "

We all chuckled but he approved the trip to Washington, D.C., with the warning that if Steve got a fever we were to come home immediately. The first night in D.C. we had dinner at the synagogue and Steve felt fine but at midnight he felt sick and Joyce was on the phone getting the first flight out for 6 a.m. The only problem was, she couldn't leave with Steve because she had a group coming in the next day for a meeting with then Secretary of the Interior Ken Salazar, a friend and former U.S. Senator from Colorado.

Joyce: "Steve was scared and I was so crazy because I didn't know what to do. My girlfriend and her friends were already on the road to D.C. Steve told me to stay and I was okay with that because I knew I would be home the next day."

Back in Denver, Steve had an infusion pump that put low doses of chemotherapy into his blood every 20 seconds, 24 hours a day, for one week. Every time he heard "swish" he knew the medicine was attacking the cancerous cells in his blood.

Steve was quarantined at home for 10 weeks because his immunity was low. He was allowed to walk our beloved dog, Muffy, around the block for exercise but was under strict orders not to pick up her poop. He also was limited to a couple of visitors at a time to reduce any chance of infection.

We decided that Joyce should go on the trip to Israel in July.

Debbie was moving back home and could help if necessary and Steve would keep himself busy doing things around the house.

> Steve: "The treatment worked. Dr. Feiner told me I have up to 15 years of remission and then I can get another treatment if necessary, so that would give me 30 years. I told him that didn't sound too good because I'm 66 and 30 years would get me to 96. I planned to live to 100!"

He's a wonderful doctor who understood our humor and how it helped us get through this difficult time. Steve doesn't talk about it unless someone asks. We never kept his illness secret from our family or the temple.

By January 2010, Steve was back full-time at the temple preparing for his last six months on the job when Joyce started her second legislative session. Among the issues to be discussed was the Colorado Sex Offender Management Board that oversaw sex offender parolees in the state. The board was up for review under the state's "sunset laws," which require reviews every 10 years.

Under Colorado's laws, sex offenders were sentenced depending on the degree of their offenses but once the prison sentences were served they were lumped into a group for parole and treatment. That meant someone convicted of molesting a child could be sent to the same treatment group as a teenager who was sentenced for underage consensual sex or someone caught urinating in public.

> Joyce: "After listening to a variety of people about their frustration with how this program was managed, I felt I needed to find out what was really occurring. I couldn't use names of anybody either in or out of the system because the

fear of retribution and retaliation was real! Their names are still on the sex offender list and do not get removed even after they complete their sentences. There are many dangerous people on this list who the public needs to be aware of but there also are ones who landed there for minor offenses, such as the guy who was caught peeing behind a tree because he couldn't find a bathroom."

Joyce, along with several defense attorneys, heard numerous complaints that the parole officers were referring a large number of the sex offenders to one treatment center. The parolees, along with family members, said the center's treatment plan was punitive and unproductive. The therapist's own website stated that sex offenders cannot be rehabilitated.

Joyce also had heard the same concerns from members at temple who were parolees or family of parolees who had treatment at this facility in question. Then she heard the same thing from a member of her extended family who, as a therapist, had landed on the sex offender list for having a consensual affair with one of his adult female patients.

> Joyce: "I came from 16 years at Jewish Family Service and when you are in therapy the goal is to improve. Here the goal of getting better was hopeless, according to the leader of the treatment center. So why go?"

For Joyce, it was clear that the state needed to check out several treatment centers for sex offenders and then give the parolees a choice. State law allows drug and domestic violence offenders choices in treatment and Joyce wanted the same for sex offenders.

Joyce: "My legislative colleagues, both Democrat and Republican, ultimately supported the final amendments. By offering treatment options our goal still was to be tough on the perpetrators and keep better track of them and also provide treatment by skilled professionals."

While her colleagues in the legislature agreed with her, everything suddenly came crashing down. Joyce feels that she was first betrayed by revealing a confidence to someone she thought she could trust. Then she did the cardinal sin for a politician speaking to a journalist: She lied to protect her extended family member.

During her 12 years to this point as an elected official, Joyce was viewed by the press as a candid, outspoken representative. But two phone calls from two different newspaper reporters turned everything upside down the same week Steve was retiring.

6

Our Stumbles
and Bumbles

We're only human

Many members of the Denver media are familiar with us because of Steve's work with the temple, the Colorado Civil Rights Commission, and on such high-profile stories as Amendment 2. When Joyce got elected to the city council she became a media favorite because she was known to speak her mind on issues.

Her 10 years on the city council brought columns of good press.

Both of us knew how to work with the media and that meant trying to find out what a reporter wanted before talking with that reporter. Steve had a secretary who monitored his

Joyce was pleased to get back into politics when she was elected to the Colorado senate in 2008. Also in 2008, our son, David, and daughter-in-law, Ali, hosted a fundraiser for future President Barack Obama. Ali asked Obama to hold their son, Bo, while son, Aiden, and daughter, Abby smiled for the photographer. Also pictured behind Ali is U.S. Senator Michael Bennet (facing page, top). Our son, Danny and daughter-one-law, Becky are active in local and national politics, including hosting a fundraiser for U.S. Senator Al Franken (facing page, bottom).

press requests. On city council, Joyce had city staff to screen her calls. But as a state senator she had no budget for staff beyond her friend, Bonnie Saliman, who assisted in the office part-time.

Given our history with the media we were not prepared to have it turn on Joyce over her work on the sex offender treatment issue. She worked for months to change the policy that was funneling most sex offenders on probation to the same company that declared there was no successful treatment for sex offenders.

Joyce dealt with the issue as a lawmaker but Steve also had heard the same issues in his role as rabbi. We both strongly support tough laws for pedophiles but we also felt there needed to be approved treatment options for offenders once they were on parole.

Advocates in the community, including attorneys, mental health officials and others, had warned officials for several years that the treatment program under question was so negative and punitive that some patients had regressed into such things as depression and even attempts at suicide.

The advocates supported Joyce's amendment proposal for the state to allow at least three approved treatment programs for referrals for sex offenders.

"We were hoping and praying that would happen," said Susan Walker, formerly with Advocates for Change, a group that includes family members of sex offenders who sought better treatment.

At legislative hearings on the proposed change to allow three referrals, Joyce saw someone from her district who testified against the referral option. She was a forensic psychologist and Joyce decided to visit her at her home to find out why she opposed the change.

In their private discussion, Joyce shared that an extended member of her family was on the sex offender's list and had gone to the one program that was receiving the majority of the parolees. Our extended family member relinquished his medical license after having a consensual affair with a female patient. When he began treatment he was stunned to learn his group sessions included convicted pedophiles and he was shocked when the program director stated there was no effective treatment for sex offenders.

Instead of helping parolees not reoffend, the program had turned into a moneymaking machine for one provider.

Joyce shared this information with the woman and told her it was confidential. But soon after this meeting Joyce believed the owner of the treatment program was feeding confidential patient information to The Denver Post.

Shortly after Joyce's amendment to expand treatment referral options won bipartisan support in the legislature, her phone rang and it was a reporter from The Post who did not cover the legislature. The reporter regularly wrote police and court stories. It would become obvious this reporter had spoken to the treatment provider under fire who would be hurt financially if the new referral policy passed.

Because Joyce didn't have anyone on staff to screen her calls she answered her phone. The reporter asked her if she had any family members on the sex offender list. She said no to protect the extended family member.

Joyce: "When the reporter called me I felt like a deer in headlights. During my service as an elected official I always took responsibility for all my actions and decisions. I never passed the buck when it came to tough votes that weren't popular. But with this issue I couldn't reveal my sources, which were many. With hindsight I didn't need to take the call and once I did I could have said no comment."

A day later another reporter who regularly wrote about the legislature and knew Joyce called and asked her if there was anything she wanted to tell him. The two reporters had spoken and he wanted to give Joyce another chance to fill in the blanks.

Joyce: "I said no, again I said no. I just thought the whole thing would evaporate."

Instead, it blew up when a radio talk show host – who had clashed with Joyce in the past over a light-rail issue – painted Joyce as someone who loved sex offenders.

Joyce: "I have six grandchildren, for goodness sakes. I want every pedophile to be appropriately taken care of; however, they also need the appropriate treatment."

The negative emails came flooding into her senate office. One read, in part: "Were you assaulted and raped by a family member or neighbor as a child? The jig is up, resign today. You have insulted the people of Colorado enough. Perhaps your husband, Mr. Rabbi, raped boys. Would that change your mind? Does one Jewish family support another if they are rapists?"

When you choose to be a politician or clergy you have to expect criticism will come with the job. We both accepted that but there also is a fine line between criticism and vicious, hateful comments.

> Steve: "Many people hold politicians and clergy up to unrealistic expectations. They think they own you and they can say whatever they want and it can be painful. We both have thick skins but there is no reason the criticism has to get so vicious."

Walker, the community advocate who had called for the change in treatment referrals for years, defended Joyce but the media continued to pounce.

"It was totally understandable how Joyce reacted," Walker said. "She just wanted to protect her family."

Joyce also received dozens of letters and cards of support.

"Anyone who has ever been touched by you publically, personally or religiously knows without a doubt your persona of warm friendship, integrity and above all your heartfelt interest and service to our city, state and the general community," wrote Ed Diner. "Hang in there gal. All will pass and your dedication to your work, plus your many, many friends will continue to be in your future."

The support helped lift Joyce's spirits but the media continued the attack.

The Denver Post editorial staff felt betrayed and unfairly reported in the editorial section that Joyce proposed the change at the last minute in the session, when in fact she had been working with different groups for six months. The talk show host spewed daily inaccuracies on his radio program that kept the rumor mill growing. David Archer, a staff member from the senate majority office, exposed the misinformation and outright lies being reported by the talk show host. The host ended up apologizing on-air for the inaccuracies but the damage had already been done.

While members of Joyce's own Democratic Party were silent, Republican senate minority leader state Senator Josh Penry came to Joyce's defense and tried to refocus the attention on the real issue: that the system needed to be changed.

Joyce: "I respected Josh and appreciated him for that."

But Josh's support fell on closed ears from the media that continued to fan the flames.

Joyce turned to our son, Danny, for advice and he helped get radio and television interviews set up for her to give the big picture of why she felt the new referral option was necessary.

Denver Post Columnist Susan Greene, who knew Joyce while she was on city council, stepped away from the sensationalism and tried to tell the entire story. She acknowledged Joyce lied to the reporters but called the subsequent reaction a "witch hunt."

"Given the chorus against her this week, you'd think the Denver Democrat had walked up and shot someone's dog," Greene wrote.

The column continued: "She's an easy target. No one gets re-elected for lying. No one wins office for being related to a sex offender. And no one snags votes for standing up for the rights of convicts – even if it happens to be the right thing to do. Politics isn't kind to complexities."

All of this was happening while family was gathering in Denver for Steve's retirement gala that weekend.

"Everyone came after her; some Democrats even came after

her and that was really painful." Danny said. "This happened right at the time my dad was retiring so it could not have been at a worse time. But when my mom gave her speech at his retirement gala the whole congregation gave her a standing ovation. It was awesome to see. I think it was even more powerful because it was evidence that the congregation and our Jewish community supported her, they had her back. Because they knew the real Joyce Foster and they loved her. It was hard to see my mom get attacked in the press because there are so many do-nothing politicians. She was the opposite. She actually was committed to accomplish meaningful things for the city and state, and she let her conscience be her guide."

"She was right on the sex offender bill," Danny continued. "The Colorado Criminal Defense Bar Association was ecstatic because the sex offender laws in Colorado were draconian. Minor offenses were treated in the most aggressive, unjust manner. And they remain that way to this day because Governor Ritter caved to public pressure and vetoed the bill. It was shameful."

Because of all of the negative press, Governor Bill Ritter, a former Denver District Attorney, ended up vetoing the bill containing the amendment on referrals. Still, he came to Joyce's defense.

The governor defended Joyce when they both were attending an unrelated event in a Denver suburb. They had gone to the city of Lakewood for the signing of another law and to support the legislator of that district. During a public comment period, a woman stood up and began to attack Joyce.

Joyce: "And the governor cut her off and told her I was a trustworthy person. Bill knew me for years and knew my heart was in the right place."

State officials also could no longer ignore the problems, and three years after the veto, state lawmakers finally approved the referral option for treatment for sex offender parolees.

Joyce: "It was a rough time but I take some comfort the program is better and more effective. The whole reason we want people to get treatment is for public safety."

The controversy also put the spotlight on the one treatment program and the director was given a warning from state officials to change his practices or risk no longer getting referrals. He ignored the warning and was removed from the state's referral list.

While that time in the spotlight was difficult for Joyce and our family the community also acknowledged the good work she accomplished as a state senator. In 2010, she was awarded the Legislator of the Year Award by the Junior League of Denver; Legislative Appreciation Award by the Jewish Community Relations Council; and A Woman of Distinction Award by the Girl Scouts of America.

In her acceptance speech to the Jewish Community Relations Council, Joyce said:

"I'm a leader. I don't take the temperature of the 'majority voice' before I take a stand on important issues. When working as a counselor I learned a long time ago that what is said to me in confidence stays with me and I could be trusted. I'm a woman of integrity and don't impugn others to make a point."

Amidst the negative press on the treatment-referral controversy our family rallied and got through the storm. Joyce went on to serve her last two years as senator just as she had done the previous two: defending issues she thought were worth defending. Her work included opposing a law that allowed Medicaid to no longer pay for circumcisions, and she spoke out against changing the term "unlicensed psychotherapists" to "registered psychotherapists," saying it was misleading.

Joyce also did not shy away from continuing to address mental health issues.

"I want to personally thank you for telling your own story about suicide in the senate committee and on the floor," wrote Susan Marine, board of directors of the Suicide Prevention Coalition of Colorado. "You helped shine a light on this very important public health problem."

She continued to support fellow Democrats, including some who didn't come to her defense during the sex offender issue.

"A friend of hers, who was later running for another elected office, was a Democrat but didn't defend my mom during her crisis," our son, David, recalled. "But my mom calls me and asks me to raise money for the candidate. I said, 'Wow, you kind of have a short memory.' She asked me what I was talking about and I reminded her that this person who she wants me to raise money for was not supportive when she needed support. The fact is, my mom turned the other cheek but when it happens to your mom, well, I didn't raise any money for the candidate."

That ugly side of politics is one reason David likely will never run for an elected office. He also says he has too thin a skin to endure the criticism that comes with the job.

"I think politics is a really, really difficult life," David said. "I have a bunch of friends [in politics] who are divorced, have strained marriages, and strained relationships. It's not worth that. I've found other ways; I raise money and I get involved with policy issues. I get engaged with issues I choose. Do I think it would be really cool to be a U.S. Senator? You bet. It would be cool in theory but being one of 100 U.S. Senators in reality can be awful: the lifestyle, the stresses, and the fights. My parents both are tough. I don't think I would have the same intestinal fortitude."

This is another place where politics and religion have something in common. Clergy, like politicians, will get criticized and sometimes it gets personal. And sometimes the clergy will even lose their jobs for their convictions.

A temple or church board hires and fires; that's similar to how the public votes its representatives in and out.

Steve: "The truth is that clergy are sometimes afraid to speak out on issues because they are hired by a board of trustees who also can fire them. And clergy get hit by criticism just like politicians and they have to be able to handle that."

Joyce: "We know many rabbis who lost their jobs because the board didn't like them. And we also know boards that won't hire a certain person because of their personal convictions."

Sometimes congregations or individuals want to push their own agendas in regard to Israel and interfaith marriage. So, if a rabbi applying for a position criticizes some Israel policies then some members of a synagogue hiring won't want that rabbi. The same with interfaith marriages: If a rabbi does not perform interfaith weddings, then some synagogues will not consider that rabbi for that pulpit.

We believe clergy and politicians need to stick to their convictions even if it means not getting a job. Otherwise, you lose your integrity and likely will be miserable. And once you get hired or elected, you need to know when to stand up for yourself.

> Steve: "There are people who think they own us. When it comes to the rabbinate, the congregation pays our salary. When it comes to politicians, the taxpayers pay their salaries. We get that, but then there are some who say because they pay our salaries they can say whatever they want about us or to us. Well, we are humans and we get hurt just like anyone else. So, I would tell anyone considering the clergy or politics that they better have a thick skin. That doesn't mean they have to be insensitive or uncaring, but you have to protect yourself or you won't survive."

Steve worked well with his board but that didn't mean he didn't have his detractors. When Rabbi Stone retired, the board voted 26-1 to promote Steve to senior rabbi. Another time a board member once asked to see Steve's daily calendar.

> Steve: "I said no. There was no reason he needed to see my calendar other than to imply I wasn't doing everything I should, which wasn't true."

While most rabbis move to a different congregation every three to five years, Steve was able to stay at one temple for 40 years – for a number of reasons. He was a very good speaker and the congregation wanted a good speaker. Not everyone always agreed with what he had to say but his other attributes – such as being there for his congregants in time of illness and funerals and being a good fundraiser – allowed the congregation and board to "agree to disagree" on some sermons.

Joyce faced the same thing: Sometimes her constituents disagreed with the way she voted but they viewed her overall record.

> Joyce: "Steve and I both knew how to navigate the daily politics and be diplomats when necessary."

Joyce thinks Steve could have taken his skills into politics.

Shortly after Joyce was elected to the Denver City Council, Steve briefly considered running for the U.S. House of Representatives in 1997. Longtime U.S. Representative Pat Schroeder decided not to run for re-election after 24 years. In 1973, she was the first woman elected to Congress from Colorado and she had a brief run for president in 1987.

> Steve: "The day Schroeder announced she wasn't going to run for re-election, David, Joyce, and I all got phone calls asking if we were going to run. And I'll tell you why I didn't. Joyce was very happy on the city council. I was not unhappy being rabbi. If I ran and won it would have forced Joyce into a decision of moving to D.C. or I would become a weekend husband. That would not have been good for me or our marriage."

> Joyce: "You would have won hands down, hands down."

> Steve: "Then I would have been a weekend husband and how much time would I have really spent with my family? I'm not unhappy I didn't run but it is one of those areas that went unfulfilled and now I am too old. It still comes up sometimes and if anyone asks, my reply is, I'm too old."

Temple Emanuel had a full year of celebration for Steve before his retirement in 2010. It is unique for a rabbi to serve his entire career at one synagogue.

But while Joyce thinks Steve would have won the election, she's not sure he would have liked the reality of how things get accomplished in politics. The reality is if you want to be an effective politician and get things done you have to know how to play the game. The public doesn't want to hear that, but that is the reality. Otherwise, you are keeping a seat warm with no real progress.

> Joyce: "Steve is too honest and he couldn't finesse the way he really should if he wanted to succeed in politics."

> Steve: "Because I see that as dishonesty. If you have an idea and you can't say it because you have to finesse, it is dishonest, in my opinion."

Voters want politicians who get things done and Steve's outspoken honesty may not have always worked in the political arena.

> Joyce: "So he would have gotten elected the first time and he would not have gotten elected the second time."

Another issue that may have hindered any political career for Steve is that some people think he is arrogant. He says that is a misperception.

For example, Steve said he never sought out attention like another well-known rabbi who had a public relations assistant. That rabbi went so far as to tell members of our synagogue that his synagogue was better and they should switch. Steve never recruited from another synagogue or called the media to promote himself. The media called Steve because he built a reputation of being forthright and honest on a number of social issues.

Steve: "People can say whatever they want, that I am arrogant and all that. I'm not arrogant. I really don't see myself as arrogant. I think when you go out there and say, 'Look at me,' I think that is arrogance, okay. I just sort of felt uncomfortable about telling people or soliciting others to promote all the wonderful things we do. I really mean it. It is just not me. If it was, I would have hired a PR person."

Instead, things that Steve spoke about often found their way to the media through members of his congregation.

When the Boy Scouts of America passed a policy to exclude "known or avowed" adult and youth homosexual members in 2000, Steve gave a sermon during Yom Kippur services that night, the holiest night of the year for Jews. He told the congregation he was returning his beloved Scout medals to the organization in protest.

Those medals included the Explorer Silver, which is equivalent to an Eagle in the Explorer Scouts, and his Ner Tamid Jewish religious award.

Steve also announced the synagogue would no longer allow the Boy Scouts to meet at its building.

Steve didn't contact the media about his decision or sermon. But by Monday, a Denver Post reporter had heard about the sermon and Steve's gesture with his medals and they became front-page news.

Steve: "She called me, I did not call her. I just never feel comfortable patting myself on the back or pointing out how great we are at temple. Others can see what we have accomplished."

The newspaper article was picked up by the Associated Press and was printed in newspapers nationwide. A Post editorial praised Steve's decision: "Rabbi Steven Foster deserves a new medal."

But one 30-year member of the congregation came out publicly against Steve. "I have the utmost respect for Steve Foster, but this is a knee-jerk reaction," the man told The Post.

Steve never regretted the decision to return the Scout medals. As a United Way board member, he also urged United Way to stop funding the organization because the Scouts were discriminating against homosexuals.

The Boy Scouts of America's National Council approved a resolution in 2013 to remove the restriction on denying membership to youth based on sexual orientation. In May 2015, Robert Gates, the president of Boys Scouts of America and former U.S. secretary of defense, called for an end to the Scouts' ban on gay adult leaders.

"We must deal with the world as it is, not as we might wish it to be," Gates said. In July 2015, the Boy Scouts of America national executive board voted to lift the longtime ban on gay troop leaders. However, troops sponsored by religious institutions are not required to permit gay leaders. That stipulation upset gay rights leaders and some religious troops still threaten to dissolve their memberships because they oppose gay leaders for any troops.

Steve is firm in what he believes in and sometimes people like to stick a label on that as being "arrogant."

Steve's sister, Syril, said people who perceive Steve as arrogant don't really know him.

"If there is arrogance or superiority or any of those yucky terms, I don't think he's meant them to be," she said, "because he is such a genuinely good person."

Syril points to Steve and Joyce's genuine kindness in times of crisis.

We remain calm and help others get through a crisis, whether in the community or family.

Our family got hit with two deaths within two days early in 2010 when Steve's cousin, Sally, passed away after a long battle with multiple sclerosis and then Syril's oldest son, Steve, died unexpectedly due to complications with his diabetes.

Syril and her husband, Bud, were out of the country on a cruise and Steve was at Denver International Airport ready to board a flight to Milwaukee to do the funeral for Sally.

> Steve: "I got a call from my niece saying Stevie had died, right before I got on the plane for Sally's funeral. I went there to bury Sally. I had no idea I also would be burying my nephew."

Joyce helped get Syril and Bud back to Milwaukee and we ushered them through the service.

"If it wasn't for Steve and Joyce I don't know how we would have gotten through that," Syril said. "That is not an arrogant human being who can also be so heartfelt."

But not everyone saw that side of Steve, and his confident personality sometimes rubbed people the wrong way. Steve always worked hard on Joyce's campaigns but mostly behind the scenes. He went door-to-door a few times and ran into people who said they couldn't vote for Joyce.

Steve: "They liked Joyce but they didn't like me. Because she was my wife, they weren't going to vote for her."

A different time campaigning door-to-door, Joyce came across a woman who went on a trip to Israel with us.

Joyce: "She said she loved our trip to Israel but she really didn't like Steve because he reminded her of her ex-husband. And I thought, oh, God!"

Another label Steve has heard is that he is intimidating.

"My dad can be intimidating and aloof but I think he's actually just shy," our daughter, Debbie, said. "Unless he has a certain task to do, I think he is shy. And my mom is not shy at all so she is often the one who made all of the conversation. That's the reason they are so successful – because she could balance out some of the social awkwardness. Even though he doesn't look socially awkward he can make people feel uncomfortable and that's when some of the confusion comes in that he is intimidating or arrogant."

Some people are intimidated by confident leaders, David said.

"My dad has the courage of his convictions and so that is sometimes intimidating," David said. "He also is stubborn. It takes a lot to convince him he is wrong to the extent he would ever admit it."

One regret for Steve: He wishes he spoke better Hebrew. We both think we probably had learning disabilities when we were young, because learning languages was hard for us.

Steve: "My Hebrew is not what it ought to be and I've always felt uncomfortable and inadequate about that. My Hebrew is just awful, awful. And that is real and truthful."

Joyce also is unhappy with her Hebrew skills, and her lack of a college degree sometimes made her feel uncomfortable, although she readily admits she never liked school.

Joyce: "I have strengths; I'm a visionary."

Steve: "She is a street savvy person."

Joyce: "I am a street savvy person and I really love people around me who are also smart and street savvy."

The upshot of us writing about our flaws is that any illusion that clergy or politicians are perfect is unfair. It also is unfair to paint all clergy or politicians with the same brush. One crooked politician doesn't mean all politicians are crooked or self-serving. Some clergy may be aloof or perceived to be arrogant but sometimes it actually could be shyness or a preoccupation with everything that is on their plates.

Steve: "I'm sure there were times, especially when you have a congregation of 2,200 families, where you can't keep track of everyone – because you just can't. I've heard people say, 'Oh I saw Rabbi Foster in the grocery store and he walked right by me and didn't say hello.' Well, I didn't see them but they saw me. And clergy, right or wrong, are expected to be that person who always says hello. You can only try your best but someone is always going to feel slighted."

But we also sometimes feel embarrassed when another rabbi or politician does something immoral that reflects on our chosen professions.

> Steve: "Anyone who engages in an immoral act dishonors the people who are in that profession. I feel personally embarrassed and will not condone their conduct."

Some members of the public also think politicians and clergy should serve as a sounding board and not disagree or question their opinions. So, sometimes we have to hold our tongue and know when to push back.

> Steve: "A business person could disagree and throw someone out of his or her office. Clergy and politicians are expected to listen and not push back."

There also is the issue of people confiding in clergy and then feeling awkward afterwards. Once they tell clergy something they are not proud of, they are reminded each time they see the clergy member.

> Steve: "People would put confidences in me and then we would see each other at parties and they would avoid me like the plague. They have projected the confidence on me and they don't want to be reminded. I would advise clergy that this projection is real. Those who confide in clergy know there is this invisible veil of confidentiality but they don't want to be reminded of it – and you have to be prepared for their reaction."

In politics, you also hear things you cannot repeat, for many reasons, and you are going to clash with people you thought were your friends. Joyce also had to step away and not vote on some issues as an elected official if there was any perception they could conflict with David and Danny's law firm.

Our family pets, Muffy, a toy poodle, and Sophie, Debbie's rescued pug, help Steve at his home office. Sadly, Sophie died in 2015.

Toward the end of Joyce's second term on city council David had more zoning and land development clients.

"There was nothing as important as her kids," David said. "If it wasn't a big issue and I had a chance to get work, she would take a walk on an issue."

David once heard rumors that a client only hired him to get rid of Joyce's vote on council.

"And I felt that was pretty nasty," he said. "That would assume they knew how my mom was going to vote on the issue, and in retrospect, that was false. And it was a blow to my ego thinking I was only important or good enough to hire to encourage my mom to recuse herself."

That also set up David to never visit Joyce at the statehouse when she was senator so no one could ever claim he was trying to influence his mother concerning his clients.

"I never stepped foot in her office the four years she was there," David said. "I didn't even know where it was. I had a client down at the state Capitol and I never wanted anybody questioning my mother's integrity."

Steve had to do the same while serving on the city's Citizen Oversight Board for the Office of the Independent Monitor if an issue conflicted with Danny's legal work representing the union for Denver Sheriff's Department officers.

Steve has been a member of the oversight board since its inception in 2005 when an independent monitor was hired by the city to oversee public complaints about the police and sheriff's departments. The monitor makes sure the internal affairs departments for the two law enforcement agencies take each public complaint seriously. For years, there was a "blue code of silence" where serious complaints often were ignored or the officers got a slap on the wrist.

But in an age of social media, several cases were recorded by onlookers who witnessed police brutality and city officials could no longer ignore they had a serious problem.

Former Mayor John Hickenlooper appointed Steve and six other citizens to the oversight board, which represents the community and keeps an eye on the independent monitor and the cases under investigation by Internal Affairs.

> Steve: "The notion that law enforcement officers, when they are accused of an alleged wrong, are investigated internally became a problem for the community because there had been so many situations where there had been egregious use of force yet the police and sheriff's departments were perceived to 'defend their own.' The independent monitor was set up so there would be an independent voice monitoring the activities and the investigations. The Citizen Oversight Board was put in place to monitor the monitor; to make sure the monitor was doing the right thing."

The board meets twice monthly and works closely with the city's public safety director, police chief, and sheriff to review each complaint. The board also takes public testimony.

> Steve: "One of the oversight board's responsibilities is to reinforce the monitor and what he is doing; at the same time, at our meetings we can say we don't think he should do this or that. It's not just monitoring the cases under investigation. The board by charter is allowed to do what we can to correct policies that should be corrected."

We know the vast majority of officers and deputies are dedicated public servants who truly serve and protect. But the bad apples must be weeded out.

In any profession, there can come a time when ethics come

into question. But for clergy and politicians there needs to be extra care to err on the side of ethics.

We also learned that while our jobs consumed many hours we had to find ways to spend quality time with our children.

Admittedly, our public lives took time away from our children when they were growing up. That's always a balancing act for any clergy or politician. We may have dropped a few balls along the way with our children but they and their families are our number one priority. And that will never change.

Joyce: "Our life is our family."

Steve: "Agreed."

7

Our Family

David, Danny, and Debbie

At the end of the day the only thing any parent really wants is for their children to be healthy and happy. As we mentioned before we are quite blessed that our two sons and daughter are successful in their own right and we're still a tight-knit group.

We disagreed at times when they were young; Steve is more of the disciplinarian, but for the fundamentals we were on the same page. For example, all three of our kids attended Jewish day school through sixth grade.

Steve and leaders from other synagogues opened the Theodor Herzl Jewish Day School (Herzl) in 1975 offsite of the Emanuel campus, with 14 students in grades 1-5. In 1979, the Rocky Mountain Hebrew Academy was established with 10 students in grades 9-12. In 1998, the two school boards voted to merge the schools into one and established the Denver Campus for Jewish Education, which now is called the Denver Jewish Day School, for kindergarten through 12th grade students.

When our children finished sixth grade at Herzl they transferred to the Denver Public Schools, which still were under a busing mandate to integrate the schools citywide. The children still attended Sunday school at the temple.

This wasn't just because Steve was a rabbi at temple. We both strongly believed the children needed that religious foundation in their lives.

> Steve: "When clergy has a family and participates in a synagogue or church it should not be for show. It should mean something to the family, as well; the kids are not just on display. They are doing something important for the congregation and they are doing something equally important for the family and for themselves. Attending Jewish day school and Sunday school are about learning personal values."

Our kids knew they had to go to day school and religious school, no question about that. They established lifelong friendships with many of their Jewish classmates.

Steve: "They didn't have a choice in that; it was our decision to make. And they went to day school until they transferred to public school. It was not only for the intellectual part but the social part too."

When they got older we did not require them to be at the synagogue every Friday night. They would have Shabbat dinners with us and then go out with their friends. But as a compromise we did require they attend Friday services at least once a month.

Joyce: "If you push on everything you are going to push them away so fast. They are not going to want to participate."

Steve: "As a clergy person I would say the same thing. I think kids have to know there are certain limits but I wouldn't require them to be there every minute of every day."

Giving them some leeway helped keep the kids active in temple without rebelling. In fact, all three of our children were active in temple and each served as president of the temple's youth group, called the Friedman Club. The group for 9th-12th graders explored Jewish worship, culture, and history as well as modern political views of Judaism and Israel.

All three serving as president of the youth group was no small matter in a large congregation with 2,000-plus families.

We were proud of our children's involvement in temple and they knew they would not get special treatment because their father was the rabbi.

Steve: "When our kids were young they wanted to come up and sit next to me on the pulpit and I said no, we didn't do that. But with my grandchildren, if they wanted to come up, they came up. They sat on my lap and it was fine. Everyone understood that there is a difference between kids and grandkids."

The children were active through high school in temple and continue to be members as adults.

"Temple is an extension of who we are," Danny said. "It's not just a synagogue for us; it's part of who we are as people.

When my dad retired it was very sad, like we were losing a part of ourselves. It felt like the whole family was retiring. That's why Becky and I felt it was so important to maintain a complete allegiance to the temple. I'm on the board at temple now. Our kids – Rex, Lucy, and Ozzie – are in Sunday school and youth group programs. We are trying to make it as continuous as possible because we think it is important."

Debbie has always considered temple her "safe place." She teaches there and previously taught at an orthodox Jewish day school in Denver.

"Growing up I was chubby and my brothers were cool and good-looking and I was definitely the odd man out," Debbie recalled. "And so I got made fun of a lot when I was little but when I was at temple everyone loved me. I always felt safe and happy there."

David also viewed temple as a home away from home but he felt the community expected more of the Foster children than others. He cites one incident from his childhood as an example.

"The Denver Broncos had just won a big game and our family was going to the airport to pick someone up," David recalled. "That was when you used to be able to go to the gate. Danny and I were tossing a small Nerf football back and forth as we were making our way to the gate. It wasn't a big deal. And then someone, I'm not sure who, tapped me on the shoulder and said, 'That's no way for the rabbi's son to behave.' So, I think I have always lived my life with someone tapping me on the shoulder or at least anticipating someone tapping me on the shoulder and saying that's not the way a rabbi's son should behave. I think I have made many of the decisions in my life around that."

Any family with two working parents knows it's hard to carve out time for your children but you have to find a way.

Steve's busy schedule didn't allow him to attend all of the kids' sporting events but we made sure we always ate as a family in the evenings. Steve would be home for dinner and likely have to leave afterward for a meeting or event at temple.

He also drove the kids to school every day before they were old enough to take the bus, and he fixed their lunches.

"His favorite lunch he was so proud of was heating up frozen pizza, and I got half in tin foil and Danny got the other half," David recalled, laughing. "Frozen pizza at 7:30 in the morning in tin foil was soggy, cold – and disgusting by noon. But he made other lunches, too, and was engaged in all of our lives."

Steve also cooked one of the kids' favorite breakfasts – "spits in the eye" – an egg sunny side up served in the middle of a piece of bread.

Every Sunday before religious school, Steve took all three children out for breakfast on the way to temple; a tradition he is now continuing with our six grandkids.

We also took family vacations each summer when our kids were growing up, a tradition we have continued as they have grown into adults. Each year, we treat our children and grandchildren to a family trip, whether it is a cruise or a long weekend in Las Vegas. The trips are a bonding time and a way to make more memories.

"The trips we took were not your average summer or family vacations; because my parents led family tours to Israel,

Egypt and Europe, the three of us all had multiple stamps in our passport before we graduated from high school," Debbie said. "This was an essential 'perk' to being a rabbi's kid." Another reason traveling is special for both of us is because family trips were limited when we were growing up.

> Steve: "We both came from very poor families and the biggest trip I ever took with my family when I was young was a car trip through the South and Washington, D.C. Joyce had the same experiences."

> Joyce: "We went from Benton Harbor to South Bend, which was 35 miles. And we'd go to Chicago because that's where our extended families lived. The first time I left the state was in 1962, a year after I graduated from high school. My family took a road trip to New York City, Washington, D.C., and Atlantic City, and that was huge for us. So, to be able to take these trips with our children and grandchildren when they are young and as they grow into adults is very special. We love sharing their experiences."

> Steve: "That's also how I feel about taking groups to Israel. I love sharing that experience with people who have never been there."

In 2014, we also started a new tradition of trips alone with our grandchildren as a gift for their bar and bat mitzvah. It started with our oldest grandchildren, Abby and Rex, when we traveled to Italy, France, and Spain in June 2014.

> Joyce: "This is the time in their lives where the children are studying both world and American history in school. By traveling with us to some of these remarkable destinations,

their studies come alive. We would listen to their questions to the travel guides on our trip and often our grandchildren remarked, 'We just studied that in school.' It's rewarding for us to enjoy two grandchildren at a time. We marvel at what terrific grandchildren we've been blessed with and how proud we are of them."

We decided if we gave Abby a check for her bat mitzvah that would be nice but a trip together would be more memorable. Abby's bat mitzvah was in June of 2013 in Israel, which was extraordinary, and Rex's bar mitzvah was January 2015. He is the first grandchild of a rabbi who served Temple Emanuel to have his bar mitzvah there. So, we decided to take them both on a trip without their parents or siblings. Just us four.

> Joyce: "Since we've set this precedent we will be taking Aiden and Lucy together when they reach the same age and then Bo and Ozzie a couple of years after that. Steve and I just need to stay healthy and ambulatory so we can fulfill our gift to our very special grandchildren."

Our relationship with each grandchild is unique right down to what David's and Danny's children call us. When our oldest grandchild, Abby, was born David and Ali asked what we wanted her to call us. Well, our children called Steve's parents Grammy and Poppy so we thought that would be fine. But Abby put her own spin on it and ended up calling us "Ammy" and "Oppy." That continued when Aiden and Aaron (Bo) joined the family.

But Danny's children – Rex, Lucy, and Ozzie – decided to call Steve "Poppy" after his father, so we are Ammy and Poppy to them.

We want to share traveling with our family because it's one of the joys of our lives. Because we were so busy with work and community activities we never really developed hobbies.

Besides golf for Steve, our work was really our hobby.

"My friends say they went hiking or camping as kids. We never went camping. My mom never would go camping. She'd be saying, 'Where are we going to stay, the JW Marriott?' " Danny said. "There are certain things I do now to get out of my comfort zone that my parents would never do, like biking and scuba diving."

Steve: "Joyce's idea of roughing it is staying at a Holiday Inn."

David and Danny have been close since they were young and now run their law practice as partners.

Another area we agreed on when the kids were growing up is that they would attend college.

More than 90 percent of American Jewish families send their children to college. Like Jewish Day school and Sunday school our children knew they would attend college but we never pushed them toward any particular career.

David graduated from the University of Colorado at Boulder with his bachelor's and master's degrees in public policy. Danny got his undergraduate degree at Indiana University. Both sons attended the University of Denver for their law degrees. David was pretty sure about his career path and also expected he would work somehow in politics.

"One of the first things I remember as a child was visiting Pat Schroeder's office when we were in Washington, D.C.," David said. "I saw that our elected officials were important and respected."

Our children also saw and heard firsthand our commitment to social justice issues.

"I also remember a time when we were in the car driving to temple and we saw a KKK rally outside of the East Denver Orthodox synagogue," David said. "Everyone else was driving by the protest but not my dad. He got out and tried to calm the Jewish people, many who were elderly and Holocaust survivors, so they wouldn't get hurt. … Politics was just part of our growing up. My dad was a very political rabbi and he still is. He's committed and he has conviction and so it's kind of natural to be engaged by it."

After David graduated from CU he worked for the Religious Action Center in D.C. His duties there included promoting passage of the Brady Bill gun control laws after President Reagan's press secretary, James Brady, was seriously injured in an assassination attempt.

Danny, well, he really wanted to be an actor, but like most actors they go to law school.

After he passed the bar he went to work for Denver District Attorney Bill Ritter. Danny later opened his own law firm where he and David are now partners.

Steve: "Bill Ritter called us and told us he was hiring Danny not because we were his friends but because he knew Danny would be a great addition to his staff."

Danny gained experience at the DA's office but wanted to go out on his own.

"I knew I didn't want to be with the district attorney's office my whole life so I started my own firm to see if I could make it. And with lots of good colleagues and excellent client service we have made it happen. We have grown and prospered and I am proud of that accomplishment. I look forward to many more years at my practice." Danny said.

Ali also works at the law firm and Debbie did a stint as David's assistant before going back to teaching.

Debbie wrote about becoming a rabbi in her journals when she was a teenager. She spent time in Israel with a group of teens when she was in high school and later during her junior year at the University of Wisconsin in Madison. She didn't go to Steve's alma mater to follow in her father's footsteps. She wanted to be near her cousins and other family members who lived in Milwaukee and Chicago.

When we went with Debbie to Madison to settle her in at the university, the first place we stopped at was Temple Beth El. She was hired on the spot to teach Sunday school.

"My dad taught at Beth El when he was a college student and for three years I taught Sunday school there," Debbie said. "It's because of his connections I got the job and people there made me feel like I was instantly part of the community."

As the youngest, Debbie experienced a childhood some-what different than our sons'. She spent a lot of time with her grandmother, Beverly, because Joyce was working at JFS. While she was active in public school and was elected to the student council at Cole Middle School, Debbie struggled somewhat

Our children celebrating after Debbie's confirmation ceremony, David (left) and Danny still rocking a bow tie.

because of bullying on the school bus and other teenage issues, including feeling unhappy about her weight.

And like many teenagers, she clashed with her parents over such things as household chores. When Debbie was 14, she started seeing a counselor and we attended some family sessions.

But those issues didn't keep Debbie from excelling at temple and in school activities. For her bat mitzvah then Mayor Federico Peña attended her ceremony and for his gift allowed her to shadow him for a day at city hall.

We later discovered Debbie, like many children, was rebelling when she hit her teens. She started smoking and the occasional underage drinking. When Debbie was a senior in high school Joyce ran for the city council seat. Debbie said it didn't impact her life much because she was concentrating on leaving for college a few months after Joyce won the election.

"I was a little jealous when my brothers were late to my graduation because they were putting in yard signs or something for her campaign," Debbie said. "I kind of reacted a little like my dad, who was proud but also wanted her around for us. But I was heading to college so the timing was good."

Her year studying in Israel during college also helped forge a new understanding between her and Steve.

As a teenager Debbie became intrigued with orthodox Jewish practices and she didn't understand why we didn't keep a more traditional home. Then she experienced orthodoxy first-hand in Israel and suddenly saw her father in a new light.

Debbie grew up in a Reform temple where men and women worshipped together. In Israel, her group went to services at an orthodox synagogue where the men and women worshipped in

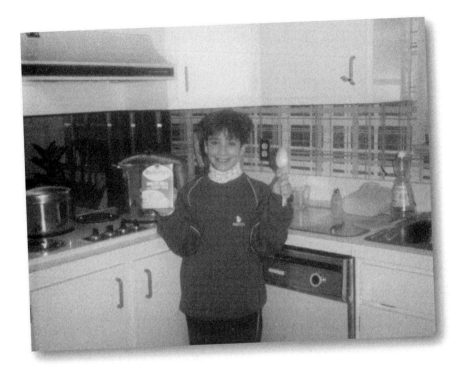

separate areas. Historically, orthodox men placed more importance on prayer and orthodox women were not required to attend the synagogue. When women did attend they were separated from the men.

For Debbie this was a new experience. She saw the men walking freely in the temple while she and other women had to watch behind an area that felt like a cage.

"All of these men were dancing and having a great time downstairs in the synagogue and the women are trying to look at what is going on literally from behind this cage upstairs," she recalled. "And I was like, this is not okay. I was not raised like this."

The group was invited to the home of one of the orthodox members for dinner. The women waited on the men and all of

Debbie, 9, is cooking with Manischewitz in our home kitchen in Denver (facing page). In 2009, she was chosen among thousands of entries as a finalist in a Manischewitz All Cook-Off competition in New York City. She won a runner-up award for her original recipe for "Mani Meatloaves."

the women, including Debbie, were expected to clean up. There also were negative comments in reference to Reform Jews.

"I had been so enamored with orthodoxy – not to become orthodox, but I had read a lot of books and I never understood my dad's perspective because there is a lot that is really beautiful about the orthodox life. But during my experience in Israel I finally understood that the orthodox didn't accept my dad as a Reform rabbi."

> Steve: "Jews are like other religions; we have those who are liberal, orthodox, and conservative. Reform rabbis often are not recognized by orthodox rabbis, although in

Denver that was not the case because we knew each other and respected each other."

Debbie's year abroad in Israel challenged her identity. For the first time, she was surrounded by other Jewish kids who knew more about Judaism than she did and spoke fluent Hebrew. Suddenly she felt, "Who was I going to be if I wasn't the expert in all things Jewish?"

When she returned to college her senior year, Debbie fell into a deep debilitating depression. She started anti-depressants which brought her out of the depression. But Debbie has always been a night-owl and in college pulling "all-nighters" is the norm, so no one realized the anti-depressants were also stimulating her first manic episodes.

Debbie is extraordinarily intuitive, creative and expressive. Her ability to manifest ideas and connect with others led to many successful endeavors in her twenties. We always knew she had the capacity to isolate but her highs and lows were manageable and did not impact her ability to be successful. She always "bounced back" quickly.

But in her thirties, we all started to notice it was taking longer for Debbie to "bounce back." Her highs and lows were becoming more intense and after meeting with a host of mental health professionals she was diagnosed with bipolar and ADHD (attention deficit hyperactivity disorder).

And Debbie, like others who are bipolar, carries on with her life while dealing with her medical issues. In addition to being a teacher, she wrote and illustrated a wonderful Passover Haggadah.

It tells the biblical story of the Israelites' Exodus from Egypt, with colorful drawings, and it has been used for years in many Jewish homes. She also has a passion for cooking, and is known for having the most creative bulletin boards in her classrooms.

> Joyce: "During Passover some of my friends posted photos of their Passover tables on Facebook and there was Debbie's Haggadah. She should be very proud that something she created is being used by so many people."

But also like other people who are bipolar, Debbie has been misunderstood regarding her medical issues. Former employers didn't understand why she was late to work or manic about cleaning a classroom. She's lost jobs and relationships and because of that she feels like she is a disappointment to her family – something we never ever felt or would ever want her to feel.

"So my brothers are successful lawyers and have their own law firm, where I did work at one time, and people know they are successful," Debbie said. "And while I am a good teacher and I have always been good with children, I've had a number of different jobs. I know it's been hard for my family to watch me cycle through extremes. I am full of potential so when I go MIA (missing in action) because I cannot get out of bed, I feel like a disappointment."

As parents we just want Debbie to be happy and it's hard when we have no control over her medical challenges.

> Steve: "It is very difficult, very difficult. And Joyce, because her father was mentally ill, feels responsible. Whether that is real or fair or not fair is irrelevant; she does feel that responsibility. And that puts an extra burden on her in terms of feeling guilty about Debbie."

Joyce never has talked publicly about Debbie's journey but she was outspoken about mental illness in general when she was on city council. The issue arose when a southeast Denver neighborhood opposed the licensing for a group home for the mentally ill. The city was challenged in a lawsuit to spread group homes for the developmentally disabled and chronically mentally ill through all segments of the city instead of only licensing them in low-income neighborhoods.

> Joyce: "This was probably the toughest issue I had in my city council experience."

Joyce got nasty calls and letters protesting the group home. She called back every single person and shared her story about her father and tried to explain the need for the home.

She also attended a public hearing where the majority of the neighbors still protested the group home. Several unfairly claimed the residents would pose a danger to children in the neighborhood.

> Joyce: "I said, okay, these people are going to be on meds 24 hours a day and there will be supervision and they won't admit anyone with a police record. The goal was to get these people back into society and get jobs. There was a bus stop nearby. I told them that maybe if my dad had this kind of place he would have gotten better. But he wasn't that lucky and I wasn't that lucky. The public hearing was at a church and I had police there because the neighbors were mean; they were so mean."

Among the crowd Joyce noticed a rabbi from another synagogue and she asked if he could help calm the crowd. Steve wasn't able to attend the meeting because of another commitment.

Joyce: "The rabbi refused. He lived in the neighborhood and didn't want the home either. So I warned the neighbors that they could fight all they wanted to and spend all of their money but the home was going to be licensed. They could not discriminate against the mentally ill any more than they could discriminate against blacks or Jews – who, I pointed out, were among the neighbors there. By the time I got home I was crying. It was disgusting. And the home opened and there were no problems then or since."

That kind of discrimination worries Joyce when Debbie speaks about her condition, but Debbie is working on her own book. She wants family, friends, and the general public to better understand and not fear people who deal with mental health issues. But she also doesn't want to be treated like a child.

"My dad pretty much leaves me alone but my mom is pretty constant with, 'Have you taken your meds? Have you taken your meds?' She's trying to fix it and she can't," Debbie said.

She moved back with us after her divorce but it's never easy for an adult to move back home. At the time, Debbie and Becky were working at the same Jewish day school and Danny and Becky invited her to live with them.

"I am extremely structured and scheduled," Becky said. "It is just the way I am. I said, 'Come to our house and you will never sleep in, I always have healthy food in our refrigerator, you will never be late for work, and you will be in bed early.' I thought all she needed was a structured home with a schedule."

Debbie appreciated staying with Danny, Becky and the kids. But most people with ADHD thrive on change and novelty, so learning executive functioning skills does not come naturally, Debbie said.

"An environment with too much structure is not a good fit and can cause friction," she said.

Debbie is too close with both Becky and Ali to let anything jeopardize their relationships.

"People with bipolar and ADHD can be infuriating to deal with; sometimes it is critical, essential to look for help outside one's own family," Debbie said.

Debbie put together a dream team: Randy Buzan, a remarkable psychiatrist; Beth Vagle, a brilliant ADHD coach; and Cheryl Newell, organizer extraordinaire.

"The most exciting part is I'm the best I've been in six years," Debbie said, in August 2015. "Something shifted the past four months and my brain is finally in sync with my heart and soul. I've learned to manage my episodes so I don't reach my tipping point; instead taking advantage of what I now call 'my manical kingdom'. Instead of depression, I've renamed it decompression – honoring my brain and body by giving them a few days to rest. I'm totally out of commission; I stay at home between 3-5 days. My current supervisors (Susan and Renee) at Emanuel are incredible. I finally found women who I could trust and feel safe with. After I decompress, I enter my 'recalibration' state – a week where I re-emerge. I'm so in tune with the signs, I can now protect myself and fend off the gigantic highs and debilitating lows. To me, it's not an illness, but rather a gift. There is genius locked inside of my brain; it has just taken me ten years of intense living (and almost dying) to finally access it."

Joyce: "Every family faces something. It can be alcohol or drugs and God only knows clergy and elected official families are not immune. It's real."

We've sat with friends who have lost children to suicide. We have listened to friends who are no longer close to their children because of family spats.

We are so fortunate that our family is close – not only geographically but also emotionally. That doesn't mean we don't quarrel at times but we usually get over it quickly and move on.

"I never feel like, ugh, I have to see Joyce and Steve or, ugh, we have to get together again," Ali said. "I've known them now for more than 17 years and they are wonderful people. I couldn't have asked for better in-laws and loving and incredible grandparents. I mean, I really feel they are the whole package. And that is something not every daughter-in-law gets to say about her in-laws. I married into this family and got a great brother-in-law in Danny and two great sisters in Becky and Debbie."

We also consider a young Jewish Iranian girl who lived with us for two years as a second daughter.

In 1978, Dalia Ashoori came to Colorado to learn English when she was 16. Her 18-year-old brother, Farhad, was already in Colorado attending community college in a Denver suburb. He had a roommate and their parents wanted their young daughter to live in a Jewish home.

Farhad put an ad in the Intermountain Jewish News to find his sister a good Jewish home. He received several offers but Dalia's parents were thrilled when we responded and they heard she could be living in a rabbi's home.

Joyce: "I saw the ad in the Jewish News and called Dalia's brother and told him Steve was a rabbi and he felt like he hit the jackpot with our home, although he hadn't heard of a Reform rabbi. We met him and he was very excited and told his parents."

Unlike her parents, Dalia thought living with a rabbi wasn't a good idea.

"At first I did not want to live with a rabbi," she recalled. "In Iran, we do not have Reform rabbis and the Jewish community in Iran is basically conservative. I thought a rabbi's home would be very strict."

We went with Dalia's brother to meet her at the airport when she arrived.

"When we got to their house it already felt like home," she recalled.

The Monday after Dalia arrived she began high school classes at Thomas Jefferson. Dalia felt somewhat as a "novelty" because there were only a handful of Middle Eastern students at the high school. Many students and some teachers also had very little knowledge of Iran and were surprised there was a large Jewish community in Iran.

"I'd get silly questions like, 'Are there cars in Iran?' People were oblivious about the country," she said.

Dalia's ongoing English lessons included sessions where she and Debbie read children's books to each other. "I also carried my dictionary around 24/7," she said.

When she came to the U.S. there were growing troubles with the Shah's government. But there was shock and fear for Iranians here when the Iranian government was overthrown.

Iranian immigrants Dalia Ashorri and her brother, Farhad, became part of our family in 1978 when Dalia came to live with us as an exchange student. Debbie enjoyed dancing with Farhad.

179

Joyce: "Once the revolution started Dalia was here with no contact from her parents and it was very difficult for her."

When hostages were taken at the U.S. Embassy in November 1979, Iranians in the U.S. faced a backlash. Joyce asked lawyers who worked for Jewish Family Service on a pro bono basis to get Dalia and her brother political asylum. We also helped their cousin and her brother's friend. We didn't want anybody sent back to Iran, because they likely would have been imprisoned or even killed.

Dalia and her brother had an uncle in the United States, who worked as a physician in Los Angeles. But we felt it wasn't safe for them to travel and we all decided they both should stay with us, and they did while tensions ran high.

Joyce: "People were so anti-Iran. We feared that there could be problems because people here didn't know that Dalia, her brother, and their friends were good people."

Once things calmed down, Dalia's brother eventually went back to his apartment and school. Dalia lived with us for two years and graduated from Thomas Jefferson.

After high school graduation, Dalia considered staying in Denver but then decided to move to California with her brother. They were working to get their parents out of the country and thought they would adjust better in California, where there is a larger Iranian population.

"I have three grown children now, so looking back I think about how hard it was for them to raise their own children and then take on the extra responsibility of me," Dalia said of the Fosters. "I helped out with their kids but it wasn't like babysitting.

It was like having three younger siblings. I felt a part of their family and that was nice."

We stayed in touch throughout the years and visit Dalia and her family in California and they visit us.

"They were my American family when I arrived all those years ago and they still are my American family," Dalia said.

We also became a second family for a brother and sister in Denver. Steve is a member of the Rotary Club of Denver and through its Denver Kids program the organization was seeking mentors for underprivileged youth. Steve's schedule didn't allow him to take on that kind of commitment. But Rotary also asked members to consider eating lunch with a junior high school student once a month.

Steve agreed and went to Baker Junior High, where he met Michael Bonilla.

> Steve: "I brought some hamburgers and we were eating lunch and Michael didn't say a word. He was shy and didn't know me from Adam. Then I asked him if he'd ever attended a Denver Broncos game. He said no. I have season tickets and I took him to a game. We were fast friends from then on."

Michael remembers the excitement of watching quarterback John Elway make one of his famous comebacks to lead the Broncos to victory.

"Rabbi Foster took me down near the field at the end of the game and I was super excited," recalled Michael, now a financial adviser and father of two. "I was shy and introverted and he didn't get a lot of conversation from me, but I always had so much respect for him."

Maria Garcia and her brother, Michael Bonilla, were thrilled to meet Mayor Wellington Webb when we took them to a Martin Luther King Jr. parade. Maria celebrated an award Joyce received for her Denver Kids program at the city's Winter Park Ski Resort (facing page).

Michael lived with his younger sister, Maria, in a one-room apartment with their single mother. Steve continued to meet with Michael once a month for different activities. After a while we thought it would be nice to invite both children to an interfaith dinner at temple.

"I remember when Michael was able to go to the Broncos games with Steve I had wished I could go, too," recalled Maria Campobasso, now a substance abuse counselor and mother of two. "I was so excited when they invited both of us to dinner and we wanted to dress up but I couldn't find my shoes. They came to our apartment and were waiting for us. When I finally found my shoes they were too small for my feet but I wore them anyway."

Michael recalls being ready to leave his sister because he didn't want to keep us waiting. We immediately noticed Maria's feet were scrunched into the too-small shoes. We also saw the cramped living conditions of the apartment.

The next day, we picked up the kids again and took them to Gart Bros., a popular sporting goods store.

> Steve: "I found Mickey Gart (one of the owners) and told him I was purchasing a pair of shoes for each child and I expected him to buy a second pair for each child and he did."

> Joyce: "We also contacted a friend who owned apartments and asked him to find a two-bedroom for the family. He gave them a lower rent, and having two rooms allowed Maria to sleep with her mother and Michael to have his own room."

Our grandsons are big sports fans: (from left to right) Ozzie, Bo, Rex and Aiden. Our granddaughters, Abby (left) and Lucy also are close (facing page). We're fortunate our sons' families live in the same neighborhood and are growing up together.

Maria recalled how that apartment changed her family's life.

"We were moving around a lot and when they got us that apartment we finally had some stability," Maria said.

What started out for Steve as a monthly lunch with Michael evolved into a friendship with both children.

We took them to different activities, including a Democratic gala in Denver celebrating the presidential election of Bill Clinton in 1992. Steve had to make a stop at the temple on the way to the party. He showed Michael and Maria a photograph on his desk taken of himself with Clinton and Mayor Webb when Clinton was in Denver campaigning.

Steve: "Maria and Michael looked at the photo of me, Clinton, and Webb. I pointed to Clinton and said, 'That is the guy who was just elected as our president.' And their response: 'You know Mayor Webb!' They didn't care about the president. They were excited we knew the city's mayor."

It became second nature for us to include the children in our weekend activities.

"We did all kinds of stuff together," Maria said. "They took us to Glenwood Springs once for my birthday and we had never been there."

When the city negotiated a new lease contract for the city's ski area, Winter Park, Joyce saw an opportunity for children in the Denver Kids program. She got the new lease operator to agree to offer eight free ski lessons for underprivileged children.

Donna Hultin, who worked at Denver Kids for 38 years, including as executive director, helped Joyce recruit businesses to donate ski coats, goggles and gloves that the children were able to keep, and rent-free ski gear for the season. They found an older bus to transport the children and adult chaperones to the ski area.

> Joyce: "We started the program to allow kids – some who had never been to the mountains – an opportunity to ski. And I didn't want it to just be for one time."

Michael remembers those fun weekends.

"I was in high school by then and I got to snowboard and ski with about 30 other kids in the program," Michael said. "That is something I never would have been able to do without the free lessons."

When Maria got older Joyce recommended her to several temple families as a babysitter and also officially became her Denver Kids sponsor.

"They paid for me to take the CPR class to be ready to babysit," Maria said. "It was great because I was able to earn my

Our family in 2015; we are surrounded with love. (Left to right, front row) Danny, daughter-in-law, Becky, daughter-in-law, Ali, David (back row) Ozzie, Lucy, Rex, Aiden, Abby, Bo and daughter, Debbie. (photo: Cheryl Spriggs)

own money. One of the families ended up taking me in as a foster daughter when my mom was going through a rough time."

Michael was the first person in his family to graduate from high school and attend college. Maria also graduated from South High School and followed in her brother's footsteps to college.

"Rabbi Foster had a special friendship with Michael and he has said that Joyce and I fell in love the minute we met," Maria said. "They have been so much more than mentors in our life; they are a second family."

Maria got a scholarship to Knox College in Galesburg, Illinois and Michael attended the University of Northern Colorado in Greeley before moving back to Denver.

"Joyce took me to college and set up my dorm room," Maria said.

We attended both of their weddings.

"When I got married, they traveled to Chicago and like a wonderful Jewish mother Joyce brought food for me on the day of the wedding," Maria said. "The Fosters have done so much for us and there is love there that is genuine."

Michael ended up leaving UNC but never gave up his dream to get his college degree. While having a full-time job and family, he continued to take classes and completed his business degree in 2015.

"Rabbi told me that anything worth having is worth working for," Michael said. "He's always been encouraging."

In recent years, Michael has helped a friend's non-profit in Denver that offers advice to first-generation college students so they are better prepared when they arrive on campus. He spends time with the students discussing such things as financial aid and answering questions.

"I probably should have asked Steve more questions when I first started college and maybe I would have lasted longer," Michael said. "I give what time I can now to help these first-generation college students, and I hope I can make a difference."

When his children are older, Michael would like to become a mentor.

"The Fosters were so generous with their time and made such a difference not only in my life, my sister and mother's lives, but the other people they have helped," Michael said.

We enjoy helping others in need and consider many friends as part of our extended family. We'll find an extra seat at our Passover dinners and our door is open for friends and their family members in crisis.

In 2014, our guest bedroom became home for a couple who are the grandson and wife of Steve's longtime congregant in Casper, Wyoming. They were in Denver for the birth of their premature son, who was hospitalized for several weeks. We knew during this stressful time our home could bring them more comfort than a hotel room.

> Steve: "The phrase that someone would give the shirt off their back really was written for Joyce because she is the first person to help anyone in need."

Joyce's brother, Jack, said she was like that since childhood.

"Joyce has always been the one who bought gifts for everyone and remembers their birthdays and special celebrations," he said. "Even when she was younger she'd have a part-time job besides working for our parents in our store so she could afford to buy us gifts."

Shopping is one of Joyce's favorite things – especially when we are traveling. She'll buy a bunch of gifts and then decide who to give them to when we return. She truly enjoys giving and expects nothing in return.

The desire to "give back" has been part of our lives as individuals and as a couple. That example has rubbed off on our children, who also make "lending a hand" part of their lives.

Every clergy and politician faces the dilemma of having enough time for everyone in their lives. We sometimes erred in giving too much time to our congregation and constituents but also always carved out time for our family.

Those nightly dinners, summer trips, and other family activities are among our most cherished memories, which we continue to build with our six grandchildren.

8

Retirement

Adjusting to life out of the limelight

We're a big sports family and Steve closely follows the Denver Broncos and Colorado Rockies. He knows the sports analogy that you should quit when you're at the top of your game.

> Steve: "It gets harder and harder to leave when you've been at one place a long time, no matter what it is – whether you are a rabbi or on city council. The longer you are there, the harder it is to say, 'Okay, I've had enough.' Joyce convinced me to retire when I did but she wasn't wrong. I really did know that the edge for me was gone. It got easy; I didn't have to worry too much. When things are easy you don't think about what is the next thing you should do. I know it was right for the congregation for me to retire. When people say get out when you are on top, I did."

What most members of temple didn't know is that there were a couple of times we considered leaving Denver. When Steve was hired as an assistant in 1970 some board members made it clear that they were hoping he would stay until Rabbi Stone retired and we liked that idea. By the time Rabbi Stone retired in 1981, Steve was ready for a smooth transition into the senior rabbi position.

> Steve: "I told the board that if they were going to do a national search for Rabbi Stone's replacement I would not apply. They already knew what I could do – my strengths and weaknesses – and if they were going to hire me there was no need for a search. But if they were not happy and wanted to do a national search, then I would go somewhere else."

After Steve had served as senior rabbi at Temple Emanuel for six years, he was recruited for the senior rabbi position at a prominent synagogue in New York City. Steve declined because he was happy at Temple Emanuel. But the individual called again and then made a trip to Denver to discuss it in person with Steve.

> Steve: "I told him I would have a family meeting and get back with him. I would not use this as leverage to possibly blackmail my congregation for a higher salary, which other people might have done."

> Joyce: "I wasn't sure what I wanted to do. It was so flattering that Steve was recruited by a prestigious synagogue and this was years before I entered politics."

The family gathered at the dinner table and it became clear which way the vote was going.

As a young couple, little did we know we'd be blessed with two wonderful daughters-in-law and our fantastic six grandchildren.

Steve: "David was going into his senior year of high school and he flatly told us he wasn't going to go. Danny was starting his sophomore year of high school and he didn't want to go either. Debbie was the only one enthusiastic to move."

Joyce: "So, we had a vote and it was 4-1 to stay."

How our lives would have changed if we did make the move. Joyce never would have had an opportunity to run for the city council or senate seats.

Steve: "While it was flattering to be asked, there is something to be said for being a big fish in a little pond. In Denver, we were able to make a difference and participate in many issues, while in New York City I would have been a small fish in a big pond. I never regretted turning that job down."

As we entered 2008, with Joyce's encouragement, Steve informed the board and congregation that he would be retiring in June 2010. That two-year notice allowed the board to begin a national search for his replacement. It also allowed the board to seriously look at what direction they wanted to go in the future: right or left; more progressive or less progressive.

"He was incredible and stayed out of the search process until he was invited in," said former board member Jim Cohen. "He never overstepped."

Steve: "The only time I got involved is when they asked me to meet with the three finalists."

The person the board chose, Rabbi Joe Black, had met us

years before when Steve interviewed him for a possible assistant position.

"I knew Rabbi Foster my entire career," Rabbi Black said. "When I was first out of rabbinical school I actually interviewed with him to become his assistant rabbi but I ended up in Minnesota. At the time, Minnesota and Denver were in the same rabbinical region so we used to go on retreats together. I considered him a great leader and a great man."

After Minnesota, Rabbi Black served as a senior rabbi in Albuquerque, New Mexico for 14 years.

"I saw Rabbi Foster at a convention and he said he was retiring and I didn't think I was interested because I had just signed a new contract in Albuquerque," Rabbi Black recalled. "But then some friends of mine in Denver encouraged me to come because Temple Emanuel has an incredible reputation as a congregation and because what Rabbi Foster was able to build here – there's no question about that. He is very out there. You know exactly who Steve Foster is: he has a big ego, he has a big personality, and he owns that himself."

But it's not always easy to follow a strong personality and Rabbi Black and his wife, Sue, discussed that before he took the job.

"A lot of people were scared to follow Steve Foster because how do you follow a legend like that? His skills and my skills are very different," Rabbi Black said. "We're very different people but we work really, really well together. I appreciate him. I appreciate his mentorship. I appreciate his leadership. I appreciate his ability to let me know what he thinks I'm doing well and if he sees me moving in a direction he wouldn't. He'll say, 'Here's something and you can do with it what you wish,' and sometimes I agree with him and sometimes I don't. We really have a wonderful relationship."

Steve purposely stayed away from large temple events, including High Holy days, for the first four years of his retirement.

"The transition was pretty smooth because Steve was very generous of spirit about it and also because he and Rabbi Black have very different rabbinates," said Janet Bronitsky. "So people can still like Rabbi Foster and get to know and like Rabbi Black. There wasn't a competition of who you like better. You could still like them both."

Rabbi Black brought different skills to the job, including a musical background as an accomplished guitar player. He's also active in social justice issues but more low-key and has given the prayer – sometimes in music – to the state legislature.

"We really like Rabbi Black but it is startling the differences between the two," Danny said. "So, if people are comparing him to my dad they are going to be sorely disappointed. But if they accept Rabbi Black for who he is then they will like him. He is a very charming, bright, talented rabbi. If the temple had gone for someone like my dad it would have been a lot harder of a transition."

Steve also had a smooth transition as senior rabbi because he served with Rabbi Stone for 11 years as his assistant. During the 10 years Rabbi Stone lived after his retirement, Steve welcomed his continued involvement in the synagogue.

> Steve: "I gave him every opportunity whenever he wanted to sit on the pulpit and he sat on the pulpit. I told him he was welcomed to do whatever life cycle events he wanted, including weddings, funerals, and baby namings."

Being a leader of a congregation for 40 years means Steve knows several generations and people still turn to him for life cycle events, such as funerals and weddings. That's where the balancing act comes in.

Steve: "If people say they want me at the funeral I always tell them it is appropriate to have the new senior rabbi there as well. And we do a lot of funerals together. I think we have come to an understanding how to do that but it was not the easiest thing. In the beginning, we both met with the family together beforehand to get information about the eulogy and it was uncomfortable. We have different styles."

We decided that if a family wanted us both to conduct a funeral we would meet with them separately and that worked much better.

> Joyce: "But that can be helpful for families, too. There's nothing more that you want to do than talk about a person who has just died. So if they have two opportunities it's great, twice as good."

On a personal level, Rabbi Black experienced Steve's compassion firsthand.

"When my father died – it was about a year after I came to Denver – the funeral was in Chicago and Steve came," Rabbi Black said. "I get emotional about it because he is a remarkable guy. That he would care enough, and it meant a huge amount to me. It wasn't grandstanding, this is what you do."

As we mentioned previously, Steve is known for his eulogies and that often means some people "reserve him" before they die. He'll get a call to go to lunch with an older congregant and he knows one item on the agenda will be reserving him for the eulogy when the time comes.

> Steve: "For me, a eulogy is divided into two parts. One is the philosophical and there are all kinds of ways you can do that. Death can be a tragedy. Death can be a friend. There's a whole series of things that death can be. Then there is the talk about the legacy that the person has left behind. So, I always try to do a little philosophy first, then the legacy stuff; and people appreciate it and it works."

Joyce also once wrote a eulogy for her dear friend, Rosie Geller, who we knew for more than 40 years. We first met her in Cincinnati when Steve was in rabbinical school. She also welcomed us into her Denver home for holiday dinners after we moved here.

Joyce didn't speak at the funeral but gave the family what she wrote.

"So Rosie, what did I love best about you? Let's start with your amazing sense of humor. You always kept us laughing. Even if I had heard the same stories and jokes a few too many times it really didn't matter. Your expression when telling them and your subtle pauses, like waiting for a drum roll as a stand-up comedienne, were always hilarious. You were always dressed to perfection: shoes, purse (too large for the mountain lodge), beautiful scarves and wonderful pantsuits. You had an eye for color... lots of it."

Steve also excelled as a public speaker and deliverer of sermons, but at times he wrote the sermons at the last moment.

> Steve: "I didn't want to have everything written out. It's one of the tips I always give to my assistants. I think

three-by-five cards are the best way to go to give you an idea where you are going. If you know where you are going the words will come out and you'll be fine. And too many rabbis are taught to write everything down. I never did that. Sermons are a spoken skill. You need to see the reactions of the people as you speak and you can't do that if you are just reading from a page."

But sometimes Steve would get caught up with daily duties and have to put together his sermon thoughts an hour before services.

Steve: "I would procrastinate and suddenly it would be 4 p.m. and I would have to get my sermon ready for that evening. That's one thing I don't miss as a rabbi. I hated that."

Joyce: "He may have been worried but I never was worried, because pearls of wisdom would come out every time. Gems."

For Joyce, giving speeches did not come easily. She anguished over her speeches when she first started running for city council and later for the state senate.

Joyce: "I would think about the speech for weeks and then finally write it. I was always nervous, no two ways about it."

Steve: "She became much better after she learned to just speak from her heart. Neither of us ever had a speechwriter."

We no longer had to worry about weekly sermons or political speeches by the end of 2012.

It is amazing to watch our grandchildren grow up and we are thrilled we can travel with them. We know these memories will last a lifetime. Family trip in 2010 to Miami; Costa Maya, Mexico; Belize City; Cozumel and Georgetown, Grand Cayman; in 2013 a photo with the grandchildren on our trip to New Orleans; Key West, Nassau and Cococay; and in 2014 a special trip with our oldest grandchildren, Rex and Abby, to celebrate their bar and bat mitzvahs with stops in Italy, France and Spain.

Steve retired in June 2010 and Joyce's tenure as a state senator ended two years later. Then we had the time to travel more. Throughout our marriage we have visited six continents, including many trips with our three children.

Joyce: "Fortunately for me, Steve is a great money manager while I'm a great bargain shopper and have saved untold amounts of money buying on sale! So I find the deals and now that we are retired we have more time to travel, which both of us enjoy."

Between our trips, we like to stay busy, but finding things that really inspire us hasn't been easy. Like Danny said, we really didn't have hobbies when our kids were growing up, because frankly, we had no time.

Steve plays golf and Joyce joined a mah-jongg group in our neighborhood, a game that requires matching domino-like tiles into rummy-like patterns. We also speak to groups when asked and spend a lot of time with our grandchildren, whether attending their sporting events or taking them as a group, or individually, to movies, lunch, or dinner.

Joyce: "I don't really have a hobby."

Steve: "Her hobby is to make sure I do the right thing."

But we still yearn to help our community. For Steve that means being a chaplain with Denver Hospice, serving on the Citizen Oversight Board and teaching a class at Iliff School of Theology. He also is actively helping with several fundraising campaigns, including Iliff, the Denver Jewish Day School, the Jewish National Fund, and his continued dedication to the temple's Shwayder camp.

He also continues to give speeches about Israel and has been an advisor to many past and current elected officials who served or serve in Congress.

Joyce also helps nonprofits with their fundraising campaigns.

Steve: "I do golf in the summer but that is less and less important. For me doing stuff – working – is my hobby. I go to the hospice and I have a responsibility. That is also why I teach at Iliff."

For his first class at Iliff in 2014, Steve invited 20 students – mostly Christian ministers – to a Passover Seder at temple. It was a good opportunity for the students to hear firsthand about the Exodus when Israelites were freed from slavery in Egypt. It is one of the most commonly observed Jewish holidays.

> Steve: "It is a centerpiece of what Judaism is about. If we don't teach Christian ministers the meaning of Passover, they don't know what it is really about."

One Iliff student brought her son, Connor, to the Seder and wrote Steve an email a week later.

"I wanted to thank you for the Seder dinner last week. Connor and I both loved it and as soon as we got into the car he asked if we could do that again next year. Thank you for including him and for providing the class such a good learning opportunity," she wrote.

Even though Joyce is no longer an elected official she is still asked to endorse candidates running for public office because voters respect her opinion. Yet she has also felt the sting of "once gone, always forgotten." Several projects Joyce worked on have come to fruition in recent years. But new officials are in office with new staffs and their institutional memory fails them when it comes to making the invitation list for a grand opening.

> Joyce: "When clergy retire there still is a very special feeling for them and they are included in many activities or at least invited. People still have special feelings for me but I wasn't invited when they had the grand reopening of Union Station in downtown Denver and that was one project Wayne Cauthen [a former mayoral chief of staff]

and I worked on to get funding. Out of sight/out of mind, and my ego gets deflated."

But that same month Joyce was invited to our grandsons' school for two different talks to second-graders about government. That more than made up for not being on the Union Station guest list.

> Joyce: "The teacher said to Ozzie, 'Would you walk your grandma to the front door?' And I said to Ozzie on the way out, 'Ozzie, was I good?' And he said, 'Ammy, you were great!' Wasn't that sweet! I had to call everyone and tell them Ozzie said I was great."

As opposed to not being invited to an event, we voluntarily stepped back the first four years of Steve's retirement and did not attend the Passover Seder at temple. Instead we had private celebrations with our family and friends. The first time we went back to temple for the Passover Seder was in 2014.

> Steve: "I stayed in the background at this Passover Seder. I was not in charge and I have to tell you it felt good, so good. Not one person came to me to complain about anything. I was just very happy."

> Joyce: "But I'm sure if we had gone back the first year after retirement you would have been very uncomfortable."

> Steve: "I just felt relaxed. My job, in part, was to always go up to the tables and greet everyone."

> Joyce: "Did you do that the other night?"

> Steve: "A little but not as much as I usually do…I used to go table to table and ask how the matzo balls were and

blah, blah, blah. That's my schmoozing. I was the schmoozer. It's working the room and I still do that, but not as much."

Steve thrives on that personal interaction and is no big fan of social media, including Facebook.

He likes the convenience of a cell phone and email. But near his retirement, he gave sermons about the negative impact of social media on personal relationships. Other clergy also have warned about this in recent years.

Steve: "I said from the pulpit when this all was beginning that I don't support it because I'm afraid what is happening is that we are disconnecting from people. Developing a sense of community and having relationships with people do not really happen online. It is too isolating. So, I find it difficult. I have people who write to me all of the time these long emails and I tell them to make an appointment to speak to me in person. You can't read another person's expressions in an email no matter how many words are all in capital letters. And they expect an answer right now. I don't do it."

Yet, Joyce wishes she had social media her entire political career because of the convenience of email and the reach of Facebook.

Joyce: "I think Facebook, if done properly and done well, is just a wonderful addition for any elected official or clergy. And I see how Rabbi Black uses it with temple. He informs people right away and he shows his lighter side. So, he can write a piece as you expect from a rabbi and then you can also see the photos he posts of his family on vacation. If used correctly Facebook can actually connect you to more people."

However, we agree that social media – if used to bully people – is dangerous. Examples are the anonymous postings on blogs that attack people or put unfair or incorrect information out to the universe.

> Steve: "People who have public lives can say they have thick skins and most do, but the negative or untrue comments take their toll and it hurts. There are people who can be really nasty and they aren't always anonymous. I've gotten lots of nasty letters over the years that are signed."

> Joyce: "I've gotten both, the anonymous letters and emails and the signed letters and emails. I agree with Steve; it absolutely takes its toll."

Rabbi Black shared with Steve an issue where someone wrongly accused him of something.

"I mean, if I have done something wrong, and I of course have missed things, but if I have done something wrong I will own it," Rabbi Black said. "I remember once going to Steve and telling him this person had accused me of something and I didn't do it and it really hurts. It still hurts to this very day. We went out to dinner and Steve told me a story about a congregant who hurt him and even though it was a long time ago, it still hurt. … It is a fine line we walk as rabbis between wanting to help and needing to help and taking care of ourselves and being strong. You have to be healthy in every way – physically, emotionally, and spiritually – because this is a job that can be very demanding time-wise and it can also take a piece of your soul. You have to take care of yourself."

> Steve: "There have been times when someone I have known for many, many years will exclude me from an important event without an explanation and it hurts me deeply. I'll wait for them to pick up the phone and call me but often the call is never made. People expect clergy not to get hurt, but we do get hurt."

While Steve still feels some slights, he learned over the years to not take most things personally. His friend, Bill Calhoun, former pastor of Montview Boulevard Presbyterian, learned that lesson, as well.

"We deal with egos and power struggles but that's the same as what doctors or business people deal with all the time," he said. "You learn to deal with such things."

While we're officially retired we never want to be disengaged from our communities or remain silent just to avoid criticism or hurt feelings. We may not be as involved as we were before, but we will speak out when we think it is necessary – whether on social justice or political issues.

Since moving to Colorado in 1970, we have traveled the state and love the Maroon Bells wilderness area near Aspen.

Afterword

As we get older we've faced losing many friends and people we admired who made this world a better place. There is less discrimination against Jews in this country now than in the past. But we know anti-Semitism exists, and often rears its ugly head whether it is about Israel or crazed individuals killing people because of their beliefs.

Both sets of our grandparents had the courage to leave countries where the Jewish community was persecuted for their Jewish identity. They came to the United States not knowing the language and having to build from the ground up.

But they had religious freedom guaranteed by our Founding Fathers. Our grandparents' struggles are the foundation of our lives and planted the seeds for our commitment to equal rights for all people. Perhaps we were destined to enter the clergy and politics because both have the ability to make real changes in our world.

And we believe that clergy and politicians have an obligation to address injustices and work toward real social change.

As children and young adults we witnessed prejudices against minorities and women that seem like fiction now to our grandchildren.

We enjoy having fun and dressing up! Our cowboy attire was for a fundraiser in the 1990s and in 1989 we attended a costume "gold rush" wedding in the mountain community of Cripple Creek, Colorado.

How wonderful that Abby and Lucy have the whole world open to them. Heck, they even could become president one day. How wonderful that Rex, Aiden, Ozzie, and Bo embrace their Judaism and don't have to worry that their religious beliefs could hinder them from living in any neighborhood they want or applying for any job.

How wonderful that all of our grandchildren – and most of their generation – don't see people as gays or lesbians but just people.

Our paths brought us to the clergy and politics to try to make a difference. As a couple we worked together to make our congregation and community a better place. It didn't always endear us to everyone but at the end of the day we stood up for what we believed in and didn't back down in the face of adversity.

We believe our three children share those traits.

"They are very well regarded and they have made a real impact on our community and of course in our lives," Danny said. "So it is a nice thing to be one of their kids. I wouldn't have wanted it any other way."

A half-century of marriage is a huge accomplishment considering the challenges clergy and political couples face beyond the typical couple.

We know we are strong as individuals but we never would have accomplished what we did without each other. Clergy life is not easy. Political life is not easy. Put the two together and sometimes you don't come out on the other end together.

But the rabbi and senator still sleep together and for that we are truly grateful and blessed.

We were honored by Jewish Family Service in 2013 for the Jack Shapiro Award for Community Service. The night was made extra special with our family attending.

Awards

We are honored that many groups have recognized our work over the years. We appreciate every single one and those that have the most significance for us are:

Steve

Faith and Freedom Award,
the Colorado Coalition for Abortion Rights, 1987

Brotherhood-Sisterhood Award,
National Conference of Christians and Jews, 1990

Humanitarian Award, Dr. Martin Luther King, Jr.
Colorado Holiday Commission, 1991

Carle Whitehead Memorial Award,
American Civil Liberties Union of Colorado, 1991

Anti-Defamation League Annual Civil Rights Award, 1993

Advocacy Award, National Associations
of Human Rights Workers, 1998

United Way of Colorado Leadership Council, 2001-2002

Spirit of CAJE Award, Colorado Agency
for Jewish Education, 2002

Jewish Outreach Institution,
Outreach Hall of Fame, 2004 Inaugural Induction

MLK Presidents Award,
The Greater Denver Metropolitan Ministerial Alliance, 2010

Civil Courage, Denver District Attorney, 2010

Joyce

Women of Distinction, Denver Chapter
of Hadassah National Council of Jewish Women, 2000

Southeast Denver Business Partnership Award, 2006

Heritage Award, Rocky Mountain Jewish Historic Society, 2007

Freshman of the year 2009 for Colorado Senate,
Independent Bankers of America, 2009

Special Recognition, Colorado Municipal League, 2009

Legislator of the Year Award,
the Junior League of Denver, 2010

Legislative Appreciation Award,
the Jewish Community Relations Council, 2010

A Woman of Distinction Award, Girl Scouts of Colorado, 2010

Guardian of Care, National Private Duty Association, 2010

As a couple

Nashama Yeteirah Award, Herzl and Rocky Mountain
Hebrew Academy at Denver campus schools, 2009

Jack Shapiro Community Service Award,
Jewish Family Service, 2013

ALLY Award, One Colorado Education Fund (supporting rights
for lesbian, gay, bisexual, and transgender Coloradans), 2014

As a family

Torch of Liberty Award, ADL Passing the Torch
for family public service, 2007

Our best award is our grandchildren, pictured here in August 2015: (from left to right), Lucy, Abby, Ozzie, Rex, Aiden and Bo. (photo: Cheryl Spriggs)

Acknowledgements

We had no idea what our journey would be like when we started this book in March 2014. We knew our stories but getting them down on paper, organized and readable was not an easy task. Often we laughed; sometimes we cried; and occasionally we bickered – and that is our lives.

We truly wanted to include all of our family and friends but it could have taken 30 years and unless we live past 100 that wasn't going to work. We want to thank everyone who took time to recall memories, including our three children, our two daughters-in-law, siblings, friends and colleagues. We also want to acknowledge the wonderful endorsements we received from colleagues and friends.

Once we had our story down, we had to get it into a book and we want to thank the professionals who helped us get there.

We sincerely wish to thank writer Cindy Brovsky for her incredible patience. Working with us was like being on a roller coaster. Between our memories, which we corrected each other often and sometimes loudly; our emotions; and deadlines, which came and went many times, she hung in there. Thank you, Cindy for focusing us and being our rock.

We also offer our sincere appreciation to custom publisher Judy Joseph of Paros Press and designer Scott Johnson of

Sputnik Design Works. They gave us support and advice from choosing the cover, creating a wonderful design, and getting the book published.

Other professionals who helped us include: freelance copy editors Jeff Leib and Susan Remkus; Chris Schneider, Schneider Photography; Stevie and Debbie Crecelius of Wonderworks Studios; Michael Stillman of Stillman Photographics; and Cheryl Spriggs/Photographer.

Our thanks also goes to Denver artist Kenny Be for providing his drawing of Joyce; Alaina Green with Jewish Family Service who helped us gather photographs; and artist Carol Ann Waugh, who helped us with a road map when we felt somewhat overwhelmed with the concept of self-publishing.

In order to get the book read outside our group of family and friends, we want to thank Christopher Loving-Campos of Inspire Graphics for creating our website: *therabbiandsenator sleeptogether.com* and Jennifer Seeley of JSeeley Consulting for coordinating social media and publicity.

We know some people will remember our memories differently but this is our story as we recall. We hope by sharing it more people will get involved in social justice issues that affect all of our lives.